MW01630188

# BATMAN AND THEOLOGY

# Batman

## and

# Theology

### Shebuel Varghese

**Published by Faith Colloquium**

ISBN-13: 978-0692603611 (Faith Colloquium)
ISBN-10: 0692603611

*For Kyle Maestri,*

*teacher, mentor, friend.*

# Contents

# *Acknowledgments*

There are a number of people I would like to thank for their support and contributions to this book. First, this book arose out of a project under the supervision of Patrick Smith, during my time as a student at Gordon-Conwell; I am incredibly grateful for his willingness to oversee my work, and for his insightful guidance throughout the project. I am thankful to others who read early drafts of the book, and offered their feedback, particularly Adam Johnson, and Kent DelHousaye. I am very thankful to my brother, who frequently listened to my ideas, and helped me to further develop them. Finally, and ultimately, I would like to express my deepest gratitude to my wife, not only for her support of my writing, but also for the countless hours of editing, and for designing the cover for this book.

# *Preface*

Growing up, Batman was a big part of my life. As kids, my brother and I were fully immersed in the world of Batman, particularly the Batman of the 1960's portrayed by Adam West, and *Batman the Animated Series*, which we so eagerly looked forward to watching after school. We played with his toys, and ran around in capes wishing we too could be superheroes.

For years, many attempts were made at a live action version of Batman, but none seemed to do the character justice. Then, in 2005, director Christopher Nolan released *Batman Begins* featuring Christian Bale, with a sequel entitled, *The Dark Knight,* released in 2008. Nolan's take on Batman was a breath of fresh air, and it satisfied viewing fans everywhere. Not only did the movies portray the character in a powerful and new way, but they restored to Batman the glory he once had when my brother and I watched him on our little television screen as children.

At the same time that we watched Batman growing up, our parents were teaching us in the instruction of the Lord and what it means to follow Christ. And as much as I was excited about Batman, I became even more passionate about Jesus. In spite of my enthusiasm for both of these figures, I never seemed to make any sort of connection between the two…until now. As you read this book, my ultimate goal is that it will lead you to a deepened love for Christ. I also trust that it will further your knowledge of the greatness of who Christ is, and what he has done.

I should be up front with my readers by saying two things: first, I am writing from a Protestant, Reformed, and Evangelical perspective. I treat what happened on the cross as historic, true, and objective, and I align my own theological views closer to the traditional accounts of atonement, justification, and salvation. Second, you are probably not going to buy this argument unless you possess a certain theological imagination, which this book demands, and may stretch at times. Nevertheless, I trust and hope that the conclusions I reach in this book are ultimately grounded in the revelation of God's Word found in Scripture.

Join me now as we look for the person and glory of Christ on the streets of Gotham City.

Shebuel Varghese<br>Spokane, WA 2016

# Stories and Theology

*"And he told them many things in parables . . ."*
*Matthew 13:3*

Throughout the history of the church, theologians have sought to explain and defend the teachings of Scripture in a coherent manner. The beauty of this tradition is that theologians are able to stand on the work that previous scholars have already laid down. Hence, the work of theology is an ongoing process. In the current, post-modern era, theologians are recognizing that there are in fact a variety of methods of engaging in theological discourse, and that there are a wealth of resources to draw from to assist theological endeavors outside of the traditional ones that are commonly used. If indeed all truth is God's truth, then surely sound theology can be found in a multitude of different places.

One of these places is in films. The cinema has become the new marketplace for theological and philosophical discussions. Given how prevalent films have become, people are indoctrinated through movies whether or not they realize it. One of the most important films in the last decade is Christopher Nolan's *Dark Knight Trilogy*. Although there are number of reasons why this is an important film (including cultural impact, tremendous acting, stunning effects, etc.), one of them is that it offers Christians a way to think theologically about what Christ has done in reconciling humanity. Frequently, Superman is the superhero seen as a Christ figure full of kindness and hope, while Batman is considered a brooding and vengeful character.[1] However, this does not need to be the only way to interpret the character of Batman, especially in light of Nolan's recent films. The goal of this book is to demonstrate that in *The Dark Knight Trilogy*, Batman should be understood as a Christ figure because he saves the people of Gotham in a manner that corresponds to the atoning work of Christ.

Before venturing forward, it is worth asking whether it is even warranted to use something that seems so remote to the Christian faith like comic book superheroes, in the task of constructive theology. This can be answered by first looking at the history of Christian thought. Historically, philosophy has often been considered the handmaiden to theology, but it had its origins in Greek and Hellenistic culture. Greek thinkers like Plato and Aristotle first formulated and consistently pursued philosophical

---

[1] To be clear, I do not want to deny that Superman is a Christ-figure. He undoubtedly is. For more on this, see *The Gospel According to the World's Greatest Superhero* by Stephen Skelton.

investigation. Nevertheless, their philosophies were later utilized by Christians, in spite of its apparent disconnection to the Christian faith, to think and speak coherently about various Christian doctrines. Christians were able to use something from the broader culture to further theological endeavors for the glory of God. Beginning with thinkers like Justin Martyr in the second century, then continuing on with major theologians of the church such as St. Augustine, St. Thomas Aquinas, St. Anselm, and then finally leading up to contemporary theologians such as Oliver Crisp, Jerry Walls, and Brian Leftow, Christian theologians have proudly used philosophical tools in assisting the theological project. What Oliver Crisp aptly says concerning philosophy might just as well apply to the comic book stories:

> Theologians have always throughout history been borrowing . . . the ideas and the concepts from philosophies that they find around them in order to underpin . . . their particular approaches to theology. So, in a sense, analytic theology is only carrying on this great, long tradition that theologians have always carried on, but it is just bringing to the discussion a certain set of tools that have not been brought into the discussion recently, and that have been kind of lacking I think to some extent in theological discourse.[2]

Likewise, given theology's history with gleaning from resources that were a part of the broader cultural context, and insofar as this

---

[2] Oliver Crisp, *Roundtable Discussion on Analytic Theology* (Interviewed by Center for Philosophy of Religion) Accessed March 19, 2015, http://philreligion.nd.edu/videos/round-table-discussions/.

is justified, it seems only reasonable that comic book stories can also provide a supplement to constructive theology.

Second, although a comic book film like *The Dark Knight* may seem like a remote resource to Christian theology, narrative is not, which is precisely what a film is. Indeed, narrative is a central element to the theological project. C.S. Lewis rightly points out, "The story does what no theorem can quite do. It may not be 'like real life' in the superficial sense, but it sets before us an image of what reality may well be like at some more central region."[3] The fact is, stories have gripped cultures all across the world for thousands of years, and continue to do so today. In the ancient western world, story-tellers were called bards, as they captivated listeners with their tales. Stories became a normal and even central part of a culture's tradition for several centuries. Among the early church fathers, for example, St. Augustine wrote an autobiographical account of his life called *The Confessions*, a narrative that is also intended to be a work of theology. While there are many prominent story-tellers in the history of Western civilization, perhaps one of the most famous English, Christian story-tellers is John Bunyan who wrote *Pilgrim's Progress*, a book that is full of theological metaphors. However, during the Enlightenment period, theological studies took a turn, and there was an emphasis on rationalism and objectivism over against

---

[3] C.S. Lewis, "On Stories," in *Essays Presented to Charles Williams*, ed. C.S. Lewis (Grand Rapids: Eerdmans, 1966), 101.

narrative and the fantastical elements of stories.[4] Thinkers like Charles Hodge and Albert Schweitzer, were clearly influenced by modernity as they were interested in the cold, hard facts of the Christian faith. In the 21st century, there has been a renewed interest in narratives and how people are shaped by them, particularly in the field of theology. Stanley Hauerwas and L. Gregory Jones write, "In recent years appeal to 'narrative' and to 'story' have been increasingly prominent in scholarly circles . . . Such appeals have caused delight in that narrative and story appear to provide a cure, if not a panacea, to a variety of Enlightenment illnesses."[5]

For Christians in particular, stories should be especially regarded in the communication of truth and knowledge for two main reasons. First, Jesus himself used stories called parables, as a medium to communicate truth. Matthew 13:34 states, "All these things Jesus said to the crowds in parables; indeed, he said nothing to them without a parable." While telling stories was not original to Jesus, it is significant that Jesus, who was no stranger to resisting common practices considered parables a worthwhile medium. C.H. Dodd explains, "At its simplest a parable is a metaphor or simile drawn from nature or common life, arresting the hearer by

---

[4] Consider for example in the 18th century, Thomas Jefferson's rejection of the miraculous in Scripture or in the early 20th century, Rudolf Bultmann's demythologizing project.

[5] Stanley Hauerwas and L. Gregory Jones, *Why Narrative?* (Eugene, OR: Wipf and Stock Publishers, 1997), 1.

its vividness or strangeness, and leaving the mind in sufficient doubt about its precise application to tease it into active thought."[6] (Interestingly, this definition could be used to explain what a film does. A well-made and proper film also arrests the audience and leaves the viewer thinking about what she has just seen, and how to interpret it.) A central part of Jesus' ministry was instruction, and Jesus understood that communicating through narratives was an especially effective way to share the message of the kingdom of God. The gospel accounts describe how the crowds gathered to listen to Jesus, and he captivated them with engaging stories. As N.T. Wright explains,

> Telling stories was . . . one of Jesus' most characteristic modes of teaching. They were ways of breaking open the worldview of Jesus' hearers, so that it could be remolded into the worldview which, Jesus was commending. His stories, like all stories, in principle, invited his hearers into a new world, making the implicit suggestion that the new worldview be tried on for size with a view to permanent purchase.[7]

If, after all, the greatest teacher in human history used stories to communicate truths about God, Christian theologians today should not feel that this medium is beyond them.

Second, the Bible itself is one large story. God reveals Godself to people through the narrative found in Scripture of

---

6 C.H. Dodd, *The Parables of the Kingdom* (London: Nisbet, 1936), 5.

7 N.T. Wright, *The New Testament and the People of God* (Minneapolis: Fortress Press, 1992), 77.

creation, fall, redemption, and consummation. To believe in Christianity, is to believe in the truth of a story about God and the world. Geerhardus Vos insightfully observes, "God has not communicated to us the knowledge of the truth as it appears in the calm light of eternity to His own timeless vision. He has not given it in the form of abstract propositions logically correlated and systematized."[8] In other words, the reason that people know God is not because God has given the world a systematic theology textbook, but because He has revealed Himself through historic events. Hence, it is important to recognize that the Bible is not a collection of random writings. Rather, the story of the Bible is an account of God and the people of God. The Scriptures relate how human beings have broken God's good, created world, but God is on a mission to restore and redeem all things back to Himself, ultimately in and through Jesus Christ. As Vos writes, "As soon as we realize that revelation is at almost every point interwoven with and conditioned by the redeeming activity of God . . . its historic character becomes perfectly intelligible and ceases to cause surprise."[9] Similarly N.T. Wright says concerning how to read Scripture, "It must be read so that the stories, and the Story, which it tells can be heard *as* stories, not as rambling ways of declaring

---

[8] Geerhardus Vos, *Redemptive History and Biblical Interpretation* (Phillipsburg, NJ: Presbyterian and Reformed Publishing Co., 1980), 7.
[9] Geerhardus Vos, *Redemptive History and Biblical Interpretation* (Phillipsburg, NJ: Presbyterian and Reformed Publishing Co., 1980), 8.

unstoried 'ideas.'"[10]

Stories have a powerful impact on human beings. When a person listens to a well-told, meaningful story, she is impacted not merely cognitively but also emotionally. Furthermore, God invites people to participate in His story through Jesus, and to discover how their stories might fit within His grander story. Therefore, it seems that stories are an important resource for Christians, and should not be ignored, as they develop and expound Christian theology, particularly in the 21st century.

---

[10] N.T. Wright, *The New Testament and the People of God* (Minneapolis: Fortress Press, 1992), 6.

# *Batman and Theism*

*"Learn to do good, seek justice, rescue the oppressed . . ."*
*Isaiah 1:17*

Although it might seem like there is nothing distinctly Christian about comic book superheroes like Batman (since one does not have to be a Christian to enjoy reading the Batman literature), the Batman mythology is most coherent within a Christian theistic framework. Jerry Walls and Felix Tallon write, "To some, perhaps, any sort of theological reflection might seem completely unnecessary for any discussion of superheroes. But the philosophical theologian and the comic-book writer aren't necessarily working at cross-purposes. For one thing, both camps are obviously interested in ethical issues."[11] Thus, in order to understand the relationship between the world of superheroes and Christian theism, it is necessary to consider the moral argument

---

[11] Felix Tallon and Jerry Walls, "Superman and Kingdom Come: The Surprise of Philosophical Theology" in *Philosophy for Superheroes*, ed. Tom Morris and Matt Morris (Chicago: Open Court, 2005), 207.

for the existence of God. The first premise of the argument is that if God does not exist, then objective moral values do not exist.[12] To be clear, objective moral values are universal and binding; they transcend cultures globally and historically. To say that objective moral values exist is to say that there is such a thing as right and wrong. Yet, natural explanations consistently fail to provide the foundation or ontological grounding for objective moral values and obligation.[13] Hence, a supernatural explanation is the proper alternative, specifically, a supernatural mind, since moral obligations only pass between minds. This supernatural being must have the power to impose moral values on human beings, and to make them feel guilty and remorseful when duties are not obeyed. It is suitable to call this perfect and powerful Being, God. William Lane Craig writes, "On the theistic view, objective moral values are rooted in God. God's own holy and perfectly good nature supplies the absolute standard against which all actions and decisions are measured. God's moral nature is what Plato called the 'Good.' He is the locus and source of moral value. He is by nature loving, generous, just, faithful, kind, and so forth."[14]

---

12 William Lane Craig, "Can We Be Good Without God," *Reasonable Faith*, accessed March 17, 2015. http://www.reasonablefaith.org/can-we-be-good-without-god.

13 For more on this see *God and Moral Obligation* by C. Stephen Evans, *Moral Relativism: Feet Firmly Planted in Mid-Air* by Francis Beckwith and Greg Koukl, along with H.P. Owen's article, "Why Morality Implies the Existence of God."

14 William Lane Craig, "Can We Be Good Without God," *Reasonable Faith*, accessed March 17, 2015. http://www.reasonablefaith.org/can-we-be-good-

The following question then arises, do objective moral values indeed exist? Specifically, do objective moral values exist in the world of superheroes? If not, then perhaps Batman lives in a universe in which God does not exist; it might be a naturalistic universe in which there is no transcendent design plan for how one ought to live, and every good deed is ultimately buried forever. Acts of bravery and self-sacrifice may be entirely worth nothing in the end. As Jerry Walls and Felix Tallon write, "If there's no God, there's no guarantee that evil ultimately will be punished and that good will triumph."[15]

However, it is demonstrably true that Batman does not operate within a naturalistic worldview, and objective moral values do indeed exist in his world. First, consider, for example the reason Bruce Wayne donned the cape and cowl and became a superhero. As a child, his parents were murdered before him, and this experience motivated him to protect the oppressed, and to fight against injustice. Indeed, Batman's purpose is to make the city of Gotham a better place, by protecting the innocent and combatting evil doers. As Bruce Wayne states in *Batman Begins*, "I seek the means to fight injustice."[16] Similarly, in *The Dark Knight*,

------

without-god.

[15] Jerry Walls Felix Tallon, "Superman and Kingdom Come: The Surprise of Philosophical Theology" in *Philosophy for Superheroes*, ed. Tom Morris and Matt Morris (Chicago: Open Court, 2005), 213.

[16] *Batman Begins*, directed by Christopher Nolan (2005; Burbank, CA: Warner Home Video, 2005), DVD.

Bruce says, "I was meant to inspire good."[17] So, clearly Batman has an affinity toward right action.

Second, Batman possesses a certain moral code by which he functions when he fights crime. For example, in *The Dark Knight Rises*, Batman sees Catwoman using a gun to kill Bane's henchman. In response, Batman knocks the gun out of her hand and emphatically commands, "No guns. No killing."[18] This behavior is also evident in other portrayals of Batman. For example, in the television episode, "Safe" of *Beware the Batman*, Batman stops a guard from killing an attacking assassin. He says, "Once you cross that line, you can't go back." When the assassin escapes, the guard is frustrated that he gets away. Batman simply responds, "It happens. That does not justify murder. You always have a choice: you can save lives or you can take them."[19] All of this implies that an objective moral framework exists in Batman's world; otherwise, why bother to do good at all? What difference does it make if one acts heroically or villainously? Indeed, such distinctions are illusory. Batman's mission to make Gotham a better place, and to do so in an honorable way, implies a moral standard by which to measure.  As C.S. Lewis writes,

Progress means not just changing, but changing for the

---

[17] *The Dark Knight*, directed by Christopher Nolan (2008; Burbank, CA: Warner Home Video, 2008), DVD.

[18] *The Dark Knight Rises*, directed by Christopher Nolan (2012; Burbank, CA: Warner Home Video, 2012), DVD.

[19] "Safe," in *Beware the Batman*, directed by Sam Liu (2013; Burbank, CA: Warner Bros Animation, 2013).

better. If no set of moral ideas were truer or better than any other, there would be no sense in preferring civilized morality to savage morality, or Christian morality to Nazi morality. In fact, of course, we all do believe that some moralities are better than others. We do believe that some of the people who tried to change the moral ideas of their own age were what we would call Reformers or Pioneers— people who understood morality better than their neighbors did. The moment you say that one set of moral ideas can be better than another, you are, in fact, measuring them both by a standard, saying that one of them conforms to that standard more nearly than the other.[20]

Hence, Batman is a reformer of sorts. He acts according to a Christian worldview because he understands that there are real and objective moral values and duties.[21] Batman recognizes that injustice and corruption need to be stopped. He possesses a sense of personal responsibility to restore peace and harmony to Gotham city, while he also trusts that in the end, good will be rewarded, and evil will be vanquished. Batman understands that what he does matters in the long run. If Batman operates according to a naturalistic worldview, then what is the point of trying to make Gotham a better place, if nothing will result from his efforts in the end? However, Batman believes that his labor to bring justice to Gotham is not in vain; it is a fruitful venture.

---

[20] C.S. Lewis, *Mere Christianity* (New York: Harper Collins, 1980), 13.
[21] While other religions such as Islam and Judaism also affirm theism and ground morality in the being of God, this is part of broader case that I am making that Batman fits best specifically within a Christian worldview as is demonstrated through his acts of atonement.

William Lane Craig rightly says,

> On the theistic hypothesis, God holds all persons morally accountable for their actions. Evil and wrong will be punished; righteousness will be vindicated. Good ultimately triumphs over evil, and we shall finally see that we do live in a moral universe after all. Despite the inequities of this life, in the end the scales of God's justice will be balanced. Thus, the moral choices we make in this life are infused with an eternal significance. We can with consistency make moral choices which run contrary to our self-interest and even undertake acts of extreme self-sacrifice, knowing that such decisions are not empty and ultimately meaningless gestures. Rather our moral lives have a paramount significance.[22]

So, Batman acts not only as a participant in restoring justice, but he also acts with the anticipation that everyone will be given their proper due in the end.

Interestingly, the character of the Joker, who is a champion of anarchy and lawlessness in the comic books, is the ultimate villain of the Batman story; he is Batman's arch-nemesis. In *The Dark Knight*, the Joker explains to Batman his understanding of morality, "You see, their morals, their code, it's a bad joke. Dropped at the first sign of trouble. They're only as good as the world allows them to be. I'll show you. When the chips are down, these civilized people, they'll eat each other. See, I'm not a monster. I'm just ahead of the curve . . . The only sensible way to

---

[22] William Lane Craig, "Can We Be Good Without God," *Reasonable Faith*, accessed March 17, 2015. http://www.reasonablefaith.org/can-we-be-good-without-god.

live in this world is without rules." Additionally, he tells Harvey Dent, "Introduce a little anarchy. Upset the established order, and everything becomes chaos. I am an agent of chaos." Even other criminals recognize the difference between the way the Batman and the Joker view morality. One of the crime bosses tells Batman, "You've got rules. The Joker, he's got no rules."[23] Evidently, the Joker acts contrary to the universe he lives in. His actions are consistent with that of a naturalistic worldview, not a theistic worldview. Bertrand Russell, the great agnostic philosopher explains the naturalistic worldview,

> That man is the product of causes which had no prevision of the end they were achieving; that his origin, his growth, his hopes and fears, his loves and his beliefs, are but the outcome of accidental collocations of atoms; that no fire, no heroism, no intensity of thought and feelings, can preserve an individual life beyond the grace; that all the labors of the ages, all the devotion, all the inspiration, all the noonday brightness of human genius, are destined to extinction in the vast death of the solar system, and that the whole temple of man's achievement must inevitably be buried beneath the debris of a universe in ruins—all these things, if not quite beyond dispute, are yet so nearly certain that no philosophy which rejects them can hope to stand. Only within the scaffolding of these truths, only on the firm foundation of unyielding despair, can the soul's habitation henceforth be safely built.[24]

---

[23] *The Dark Knight*, directed by Christopher Nolan (2008; Burbank, CA: Warner Home Video, 2008), DVD.
[24] Bertrand Russell, "A Free Man's Worship," in *Why I Am Not a Christian* (London: Allen and Unwin, 1957), 107.

This is undeniably a dark picture of the universe because there are no objective truths about right or wrong, or good or evil, and the universe is alone, heading into extinction. Disturbingly, this way of thinking is consistent with the actions of the Joker. In other words, the Joker's deeds are merely the logical outworking of his own belief system. If the moral code is simply a "bad joke," then ethical behavior is irrelevant. Although the Joker commits heinous atrocities, like blowing up a hospital, and burning a man alive, he does not consider himself to be a moral monster; he is the truest expression of a sociopath.

In contrast to the Joker's worldview, the Christian worldview affirms the reality of good and evil. Moreover, it states that human beings are morally fallen creatures who have deviated from the good, introducing brokenness and injustice to this world. The need therefore is to solve the problem of evil, and to get human beings back on the right track. This is precisely what Christ does, and this is precisely what the atonement is about.

# *The Atonement*

*"All this is from God, who reconciled us to himself through Christ . . ."*
*1 Timothy 1:15*

So, how is Batman like Jesus? How do Batman's actions as a superhero in any way correspond to Christ's atoning work on the cross? In order to properly answer these questions, it is suitable to briefly explain what Christians mean when they talk about the atonement. In the words of James Beilby and Paul Eddy, "Broadly speaking, the term *atonement* . . . refers to a reconciled state of 'at-one-ness' between parties that were formerly alienated in some manner."[25] According to the Christian narrative, the Triune God and created humanity are the two parties who are alienated from each other. In order to bring reconciliation, an act of atonement takes place. Wayne Grudem writes, "The atonement is the work Christ did in his life and death to earn our salvation."[26] Similarly, Michael Rea writes,

Traditional Christianity maintains that human beings are

---

[25] James Beilby and Paul Eddy, "The Atonement: An Introduction" in *The Nature of the Atonement: Four Views*, ed. James Beilby and Paul Eddy (Downers Grove, IL: IVP Academic, 2006), 9.
[26] Wayne Gruden, *Systematic Theology* (Grand Rapids: Zondervan, 1994), 568.

subject to death and eternal separation from God as a result of their sinfulness, but that they can be saved from this condition somehow as a result of what we might refer to as 'the work of Jesus', which work includes at least his suffering and death on the cross, and perhaps also his sinless life, resurrection, and ascension.[27]

Hence, broadly speaking, the doctrine of atonement concerns bringing about reconciliation. Specifically, atonement refers to what the person of Jesus Christ did to achieve reconciliation. As the apostle Paul writes, "While we were God's enemies, we were reconciled to him through the death of his Son."[28]

The question then follows, how did this reconciliation through the cross take place? In other words, what happened on the cross that brought about this new state of reality? How did the life and death of Christ function to make things right again? These are essential questions that Christian theologians have grappled with for many years, and they propose alternate theories (or models) throughout church history. Although there are a number of significant theories of atonement (some of which are more biblically warranted than others), three are particularly relevant to the Batman narrative. First, there is the Christus Victor theory of atonement.[29] According to the Christus Victor model, Christ's life

---

[27] Michael Rea, "Philosophy and Christian Theology," *Stanford Encyclopedia of Philosophy*, accessed March 17, 2015.
http://plato.stanford.edu/entries/christiantheology-philosophy/
[28] Rom. 5:10 (NIV).
[29] This view was particularly popular among the church father like Irenaeus, Gregory of Nyssa, Athanasius, and John of Damascus. It went through a

and death brought about restoration through the defeat of the powers of evil, like Satan, sin, and death. Gustaf Aulen writes,

> This type of view may be described provisionally as the 'dramatic.' Its central theme is the idea of the Atonement as a Divine conflict and victory; Christ—Christus Victory— fights against and triumphs over the evil powers of the world, the tyrants under which humankind is in bondage and suffering, and in Him God reconciles the world to Himself.[30]

This model emphasizes the oppression that human beings are under due to the powers and authorities of evil. Consequently, what Christ does on the cross is to battle and conquer the forces of evil, thereby liberating humanity and bringing about reconciliation.

Second, many evangelical theologians hold to the penal substitution model of atonement.[31] According to this model, Christ, although innocent, pays the price on behalf of sinners by receiving their penalty. Thomas Schreiner writes,

> The Father because of his love for human beings, sent his Son (who offered himself willingly and gladly) to satisfy God's justice, so that Christ took the place of sinners. The punishment and penalty we deserved was laid on Jesus Christ instead of us, so that in the cross both God's holiness and love are manifested.[32]

---

serious decline in the middle ages, when Anselm proposed his satisfaction theory of atonement. However, there has been a resurgence of interest in the Christus Victor model among theologians and biblical scholars particularly since Gustaf Aulen's work, *Christus Victor* published in 1931.

[30] Gustaf Aulen, *Christus Victor* (London: SPCK, 1931), 4.

[31] Penal substitution has its roots in Anselm's satisfaction theory, but is distinct enough from it that it is in fact its own model. It is especially popular

In contrast to the Christus Victor model, which emphasizes that humans are under the oppression of Satan, the penal substitution model regards human beings as personally sinful, and thus deserving of judgment before a just God. Jesus stands in the place of sinners and bears the weight of judgment, satisfying God's justice, and bringing about reconciliation.

Finally, there is the moral exemplar theory of atonement.[33] According to this view, the problem is that human beings are in a state of ethical and spiritual failure, and consequently in need of moral reform. So, God atones for the sins of humanity by offering Jesus as an example of love through his life, teachings, and ultimately his death on the cross. Christ's life, teachings, and sacrificial death atone for sins, in that they inspire people to love and sacrifice in a transformative way. Philip Quinn writes, "On [this] view, the love of God for us exhibited in the life of Christ is a good example to imitate, but it is not merely an example. Above and beyond its exemplary value, there is in it a surplus of mysterious causal efficacy that no merely human love possesses."[34] Unlike penal substitution which considers Christ's

---

among Reformed thinkers like John Calvin, J.I. Packer, and Wayne Grudem, and it continues to be the dominant way of understanding Christ's death among Protestant evangelicals.

32 Thomas Schreiner, "Penal Substitution View" in *The Nature of the Atonement: Four Views,* ed. James Beilby and Paul Eddy (Downers Grove, IL: IVP Academic, 2006), 68.

33 This view has its roots in the early church fathers, but its most prominent advocate is Peter Abelard.

34 Philip Quinn, "Abelard on Atonement: 'Nothing Unintelligible, Arbitrary,

work primarily in terms of paying the penalty of sinners or Christus Victor with its focus on the liberation from the evil powers, the moral exemplar view emphasizes Christ as an example and inspiration to sinful people to live moral and loving lives.

At least on the surface level, there is nothing incompatible between these three models of atonement. In fact, they are complementary to one another. After all, if more than one model is required to provide a more satisfying explanation of what happened on the cross, why not use as many as necessary? Indeed, the New Testament writers use a variety of ways to describe what happened when Christ died, such as, to display God's amazing love (John 3:16), to defeat Satan (Hebrews 2:14-15), to pay the penalty of sin (Romans 4:25), and so on. Concerning the different ways the Bible describes the atonement, Trevor Hart rightly says, "The metaphors are not to be understood as exchangeable, as if one might simply be substituted for another without net gain or loss, but complementary, directing us to distinct elements in and consequences of the fullness of God's saving action in Christ and the Spirit."[35] Hence, there is a unity and diversity to Christ's atoning work. The different motifs of the atonement should not be ignored, rather, they should be consistently highlighted so as

---

Illogical, or Immoral about It'," in *Reasoned Faith: Essays in Philosophical Theology in Honor of Norman Kretzmann,* ed. Eleonore Stump (Ithaca, NY: Cornell University Press,1993), 153.

[35] Trevor Hart, "Redemption and Fall" in *The Cambridge Companion to Christian Doctrine,* ed. Colin Gunton 168.

not to forget the greatness of what Christ accomplished. Hence, Nolan's *Dark Knight Trilogy* is significant because it illuminates these different motifs. As Batman atones for the transgressions of Gotham, he demonstrates the different theories found in the Christian doctrine of atonement.

# Batman Begins: Standing in the Gap

*"There is also one mediator between God and humankind,*
*Christ Jesus, himself . . ."*
*1 Timothy 2:5*

*Batman Begins* first introduces Bruce Wayne as a young boy in Gotham who belongs to very wealthy parents, Thomas and Martha Wayne. Although the city is riddled with crime, corruption, and poverty, Thomas and Martha Wayne remain noble and generous citizens, and they try to do good deeds for the city through their company, Wayne Enterprises. One evening, while the family is walking through an alley, Bruce's parents are shot before him by a mugger. Bruce lives with anger and fear for several years afterward because of his parents' death. He is also disgusted by the corruption of Gotham, but he feels powerless to do anything. He ultimately decides to travel the world, and to learn about the criminal lifestyle. He eventually ends up in a prison somewhere in Asia, where a man named Henri Ducard visits him. The mysterious visitor tells Bruce that he recognizes how much Bruce wants to stop criminality and serve true justice. Ducard invites Bruce to train with Ra's Al Ghul and The League of Shadows, a secret society who enforces strict justice. Bruce trains with The League of Shadows, but he is disturbed by their legalistic and extreme methods such as killing persons who commit moderate crimes. Bruce also learns that Ra's Al Ghul wants him to lead The League of Shadows back to Gotham and to destroy the city because of its total corruption. However, Bruce escapes, and he discovers that his calling is to rid Gotham of corruption by taking on another persona: the Batman. As the caped crusader, Bruce enlists the help of police sergeant, James Gordon, research scientist, Lucius Fox, and his personal butler, Alfred Pennyworth. As Batman patrols the streets, he discovers plans of an aerosol toxin that induces extreme fears and hallucinations to be released in Gotham. With the help of Lucius Fox, Batman creates an antidote, only to discover that Henri Ducard, who is in fact Ra's Al Ghul, has come to Gotham with the League of Shadows in order to destroy the city with the toxin. Batman ultimately stops Ra's Al Ghul, and keeps Gotham safe.[36]

## Atonement in *Batman Begins*

The city of Gotham is much like humanity; it represents the people whom God has created in his image and loves. The book of Genesis describes the special bond God initially shared

---

[36] *Batman Begins*, directed by Christopher Nolan (2005; Burbank, CA: Warner Home Video, 2005), DVD.

with human beings; he even walked with Adam and Eve.[37] However, the story of Genesis goes on to describe how evil and sin enter the world through human beings' own corruption.[38] In his work, *On the Incarnation*, St. Athanasius writes, "Instead of remaining in the state in which God had created them, they were in process of becoming corrupted entirely, and death had them completely under its dominion."[39] This is also the case with Gotham. Evidently, at some point, Gotham was a great and beautiful city; it was not always polluted with wickedness. In fact, there still exists very small pockets that reflect the greatness that Gotham once was, represented by people like Thomas and Martha Wayne, or even some of the city's beautiful architecture. However, Gotham is currently in a state of corruption. It is full of criminality, injustice, and disorder, and it is under the dominion of mob bosses and corrupt bureaucrats. Athanasius' words apply quite well to the city of Gotham: "Thefts were everywhere, murder and rapine filled the earth, law was disregarded in corruption and injustice, all kinds of iniquities were perpetrated by all, both single and in common."[40] Ra's Al Ghul emphatically states that Gotham is beyond saving, and must be allowed to die.[41] Indeed, the phrase

---

[37] Gen. 1:27 (NRSV).

[38] Gen. 3 (NRSV).

[39] St. Athanasius, *On the Incarnation*, (Crestwood, NY: St. Vladmir's Seminary Press, 1946), 29.

[40] Ibid.

[41] *Batman Begins*, directed by Christopher Nolan (2005; Burbank, CA: Warner Home Video, 2005), DVD.

"allowed to die" is fitting as Gotham is on due course to death and destruction as a result of its own evil and corruption. As Paul writes, "The wages of sin is death."[42] Similarly, Karl Barth writes concerning the world, "It has fallen, it is rushing headlong into nothingness, into eternal death. Of itself it is not capable of any counter-movement to arrest this fall."[43] Therefore, the city of Gotham serves as a sort of microcosm for the whole of humanity. It represents the broken and sinful world.[44]

Nevertheless, Bruce Wayne still loves the people of Gotham. He does not believe that the city is beyond saving, and he thinks that Gotham can be redeemed. Surprisingly and strangely, although he is a billionaire businessman who travels the world and lacks nothing, Bruce Wayne still has a special bond with the people of the city. He cherishes Gotham city, and he hates that it is in shambles. In fact, he desires to see it restored, and he himself becomes the restorer of Gotham. (Arguably, he is the only one who has the power to restore the city because no one else in

---

[42] Romans 6:23 (NRSV)

[43] Karl Barth, *CD* IV.1 (Peabody, MA: Hendrickson Publishers, 1956), 213.

[44] It should be noted that in Christian theology, sin is first and foremost committed against God, thereby creating the need for reconciliation between God and humanity. However, in Gotham the problem is not created by transgressions committed against a perfect God. Rather, the crimes are against other human persons. The problem in Gotham is the horizontal, rather than vertical dimension of sin. Hence, Batman's goal is to bring harmony and justice amongst the people of Gotham. Nevertheless, for the sake of this argument the point is that in both Christian theology and in the Batman story, there is a serious problem that both God and Batman provide a solution for, and that problem is human transgression.

Gotham possesses the resources, moral authority, and love, to accomplish the salvation of the people.) When asked why he is returning to Gotham, Bruce responds, "I want to show the people of Gotham that their city does not belong to the criminals and the corrupt."[45] Bruce believes that while the city is permeated with injustice, it is also under oppression and bondage as it currently "belongs to the criminals and corrupt." Evidently, Bruce has compassion on the people of Gotham who are in the grips of corruption. So, Bruce Wayne chooses to take on the act of restoration for two reasons: first, because he loves the city and the people of Gotham, and second, because he loves justice and harmony. Hence, Bruce Wayne/Batman acts like God; and specifically like Jesus Christ. John 3:16 says, "For God so loved the world that He gave His only Son . . ." and Paul writes in Ephesians, "But God, being rich in mercy, because of the great love with which he loved us even when we were dead in our trespasses, made us alive together with Christ."[46] Since human beings are created in the divine image, they are unique among creation. Humans have a special place in God's heart; God's desire for redeeming humankind arises from his deep love for human beings. As James Garrett writes, "The love of God is the motive for the saving work of Jesus Christ as the Son of God. Jesus died

---

[45] *Batman Begins*, directed by Christopher Nolan (2005; Burbank, CA: Warner Home Video, 2005), DVD.
[46] Eph. 2:4-5 (NASB).

not to purchase, obtain, or secure the love of God, but in dying for the salvation of human beings Jesus revealed or demonstrated the self-giving love of the Father."[47]

Additionally, God redeems humanity because of his love for justice. Paul writes, "Through the redemption of Christ Jesus, whom God put forward . . . He did this to show his righteousness."[48] Moreover, since God is the greatest possible being, he is all good, and possesses no moral imperfections. Consequently, an all-good God hates evil and injustice, and loves righteousness and harmony. As Stephen Davis writes, "Loving the good is an essential property of any moral being. Hating the evil is in effect an accidental property of a moral being, since it depends on the existence of evil. Still, in the presence of evil, a moral being like God will hate and oppose it."[49]  In the act of atonement, God obliterates evil and injustice because he desires to see peace and harmony restored to the earth, thereby revealing his righteous and morally perfect nature. This is precisely what Batman does; due to his love for justice, he opposes wickedness, and pours out his wrath on evildoers.

Although God owes nothing to fallen humanity, and could simply step back as the world tears itself apart, God chooses to

---

[47] James Leo Garrett, *Systematic Theology: Volume 2* (Grand Rapids: Wm B. Eerdmans Publishing Co., 1995), 33.
[48] Rom. 3:25 (NRSV).
[49] Stephen Davis, *Christian Philosophical Theology* (New York: Oxford University Press, 2006), 216.

save humanity. As Karl Barth says, "He loved the world of men, but He did not need to continue to love the sinful world of men. We can only say that He has actually done so."[50] Similarly, Wayne Grudem writes,

> It is important to realize that it was not necessary for God to save any people at all. When we appreciate that "God did not spare the angels when they sinned, but cast them into hell and committed them to pits of nether gloom to be kept until the judgment" (2 Peter 2:4), then we realize that God could also have chosen with perfect justice to have left us in our sins awaiting judgment: he could have chosen to save no one, just as he did with the sinful angels.[51]

God is therefore totally free and totally just to act however he pleases. Yet, the New Testament reveals that God freely chose to intervene and sink into the depths of the world in Jesus. As Philippians 2:5-7 says concerning Jesus, "who, though he was in the form of God, did not count equality with God a thing to be grasped, but emptied himself, by taking the form of a servant, being born in the likeness of men. And being found in human form, he humbled himself by becoming obedient to the point of death, even death on a cross." Here lies another parallel between Christ and Batman. Like the pre-incarnate Christ, Bruce Wayne possesses all the riches and glories imaginable. Bruce lives in Wayne Manor on a large and beautiful estate, he drives fast and

---

[50] Karl Barth, *CD* IV.1 (Peabody, MA: Hendrickson Publishers, 1956), 80.
[51] Wayne Gruden, *Systematic Theology* (Grand Rapids: Zondervan, 1994), 569.

luxurious cars, and people serve him all day. He has seemingly infinite resources, and he possesses great wealth and prestige. Bruce comes from an honorable and a lofty place. Carmine Falcone, one of the crime bosses in the city, reminds Bruce of his position of incredible privilege, "You are the prince of Gotham. You would have to go a thousand miles for someone not to know your name."[52] If Bruce wanted to, he could simply live a comfortable and luxurious life that is free of pain, humiliation, and servitude. Yet, due to his love for justice and the people of Gotham, he chooses to sink down into the filth and crime of the city, just as Jesus, the prince of heaven, steps down from the throne of glory, and humbly walks into a sin-filled world. It is important to note that God is totally free in his act of redemption; Jesus willingly chooses to sacrifice himself for human beings. As Jesus says, "I lay down my life . . . No one takes it from me, but I lay it down of my own accord. I have authority to lay it down, and I have authority to take it up again."[53] Similarly, in the opening of *Batman Begins*, Bruce is in a prison camp, but he is there by choice, not because he is forced to be there. On the surface it may seem as if Bruce is not in control, but in fact he possesses all the authority. He is the owner of Wayne Enterprises, and the sole heir to one of the wealthiest and most powerful families in the world.

---

[52] *Batman Begins*, directed by Christopher Nolan (2005; Burbank, CA: Warner Home Video, 2005), DVD.

[53] John 10:17-18 (NIV).

As Henri Ducard rightfully states, "Someone like you is only here by choice." Bruce Wayne is self-determined. No one forces him to put himself in dirty and painful situations; by his own volition, he fights to restore justice and save the city.

How then does Batman go about restoring Gotham city? In other words, how does the atonement take place? First, Batman disempowers the illegitimate authorities and unjust forces. Bruce understands that one of the primary reasons that Gotham is in a terrible state is because it is under the oppression of crime bosses and mobsters. In Gotham, the most powerful crime boss is Carmine Falcone. As a young man, Bruce confronts Falcone in a restaurant, and Falcone pulls out his gun and says, "Look around you: you'll see two councilmen, a union official, a couple off-duty cops, and a judge. Now, I wouldn't have a second's hesitation of blowing your head off right here and right now in front of 'em. That's power you can't buy! That's the power of fear!" Falcone holds the people of Gotham in his clenches, and rules over them through fear. In spite of the so called law enforcers around him, Falcone is the man who is truly in charge. He pays people off and intimidates others through violent threats. He tells psychiatrist, Jonathan Crane, "I own the muscle in this town." When later threatened that Ra's Al Ghul will lock him up, Falcone responds, "Not even he can keep me locked up. Not in my town."[54]

---

[54] *Batman Begins*, directed by Christopher Nolan (2005; Burbank, CA: Warner Home Video, 2005), DVD.

Evidently, Gotham is in the grip of Carmine Falcone and others who work with him, and Falcone knows it. So, as Batman's first act in Gotham, he takes down Carmine Falcone from his position of oppressive power. Batman's first appearance is at the docks where Falcone's men are loading drugs. Carmine Falcone attempts to flee in his car, but to no avail. Batman pulls him out of his car, knocks him unconscious, and ties him to a floodlight for everyone to see to him. This scene powerfully portrays what Paul writes in Colossians 2, "He disarmed the rulers and authorities and made a public example of them, triumphing over them in it." Carmine Falcone is like those whom Paul calls the "rulers and authorities" or "principalities and powers."[55] The New Testament writers believed that humanity is in bondage to evil forces. Jesus desires to see people liberated, and to no longer live in fearful bondage. As Gustaf Aulen writes,

> Paul regards men as held in bondage under objective powers of evil; namely, first of all, the 'flesh,' sin, the Law, death. These are no mere abstract or metaphorical expressions, but *Wesenheiten*, realities, active forces. Secondly, Paul speaks of another order of powers of evil, demons, principalities, powers, which bear rule in this world, God having permitted them for the time being to have dominion…The purpose of Christ's coming is to deliver people from all these powers of evil.[56]

On the cross, therefore, Jesus releases humanity from the grip of

---

[55] Col. 2:15 (NRSV).
[56] Gustaf Aulen, *Christus Victor* (London: SPCK, 1931), 65.

evil. The dark powers engage in battle with Jesus at Calvary, however, Jesus emerges triumphant, and conquers and humiliates the evil powers. Christ was the victor on the cross by stripping the rulers of their powers and exposing them for all to witness their defeat. This is precisely what Batman does with Carmine Falcone. Although Falcone, like the dark powers of evil, holds people in his grips and rules over them with oppression and fear, Batman confronts him head-on, and renders him powerless, tying and shaming him, so that the people of Gotham know that they do not need to live under the terror of Falcone. They are now liberated to live righteously because the corrupt powers of evil have been defeated.

Second, Batman becomes a mediating representative of the people of Gotham, and stands between them and oncoming destruction. In *Batman Begins*, Ra's Al Ghul commits himself to strict justice. He shows no compassion, and no mercy. He believes in the strict order of the law. During Bruce Wayne's training under Ra's Al Ghul, he is shown a criminal in a cage. Bruce asks, "What will happen to him?" to which Ra's Al Ghul responds, "Justice. Crime cannot be tolerated." Before he allows Bruce Wayne to enter his League of Shadows, Ra's commands Bruce to kill the criminal, saying, "First you must prove your commitment to justice…your compassion is a weakness your enemies will not share." Bruce refuses, and escapes back to Gotham to patrol the city. Eventually, Ra's Al Ghul comes to Gotham to ensure personally that the city is destroyed because of how corrupt it is. Ra's reveals his plan to Bruce that he intends to destroy the city. Bruce says, "You're going to destroy millions of lives." Ra's responds "Crime, despair... this is not how man was supposed to live. The League of Shadows has been a check against human corruption for thousands of years. We sacked Rome, loaded trade ships with plague rats, burned London to the ground. Every time a civilization reaches the pinnacle of its decadence, we return to restore the balance." When Bruce retorts that Gotham is not beyond saving, Ra's says, "You are defending a city so corrupt, we have infiltrated every level of its infrastructure."[57] Ra's shows no mercy, and does not possess the slightest amount of compassion for law-breakers.

It might be tempting to think that Ra's Al Ghul is like God the Father, full of wrath and retribution, demanding satisfaction for justice, but this comparison is deeply misguided. To be fair, there are some points of similarity between Ra's and God the Father. Both do not tolerate injustice and seek to get rid of it. Both demand perfect and upright living. Both are indignant about the evil in the world. However, to equate God the Father to Ra's is ultimately mistaken. First, Ra's Al Ghul is the villain of the story; God the Father is not the villain in Christianity. This would be some variation of Marcionism which taught that the God of the

---

[57] *Batman Begins*, directed by Christopher Nolan (2005; Burbank, CA: Warner Home Video, 2005), DVD.

Hebrew Bible was evil, while Jesus is the loving savior. Additionally, Ra's fights Batman and ultimately loses. God the Father is not at war with Jesus the Savior. Or to put it more directly, God does not act in conflict with Godself. As Adonis Vidu writes, "Any ascription of action to God must render his agency as fully consistent with itself and unified."[58] So, there is no disunity in God where the Father wants to destroy humanity, and Jesus pleads with him to stop. Indeed, the New Testament indicates that God the Father is not intent on destruction, rather he seeks to save. As John 3:17 says, "He did not send his Son into the world to condemn the world, but that through him the world might be saved." The one will of the Triune God works together in harmony at the atonement. God the Father is as much an active agent in the saving work of humanity as is the Son.  (If anything, God the Father is most like Thomas Wayne, Bruce Wayne's own father. Indeed, it is through Bruce's father that he receives his authority and status. Bruce's father models someone who lives in service and sacrifice to the people of Gotham. He also wants to see Gotham restored. In a way, Bruce feels like he is carrying on his father's legacy, or doing the will of his father, so to speak. As Rachel tells Bruce, "Your father would be very proud of you."[59] This statement is reminiscent of the proclamation of God in the

---

[58] Adonis Vidu, *Atonement, Law, and Justice* (Grand Rapids: Baker Academic, 2014), 258.

[59] *Batman Begins*, directed by Christopher Nolan (2005; Burbank, CA: Warner Home Video, 2005), DVD.

gospels, "This is my Son in whom I am well pleased."[60]) Finally, unlike God the Father, Ra's Al Ghul possesses no mercy. His only goal is to see if people measure up to the law, and to accuse and destroy them if they do not.

Since Ra's is not like God the Father, who then does he represent? Ra's Al Ghul best serves as a depiction of the power of the law, and of Satan. Ra's Al Ghul is bent on absolute justice. He personifies the law, and he sees it as his duty to uphold the strict moral code, regardless of how it affects people. The law is a sort of blind guide to simply see how people measure up to its standard, and it judges all who fail to meet its standard. Laws exist for people to obey in order to maintain goodness and order; they are unprejudiced, and absolute. The apostle Paul writes in Romans 2, "All who have sinned under the law will be judged by the law,"[61] and in Romans 4, Paul goes on to say, "The law brings wrath."[62] In Galatians, Paul quotes Deuteronomy, and says, "Cursed is everyone who does not observe and obey all the things written in the book of the law."[63] As Doug Moo comments on the role of the law, "Rather than rescuing people from the sentence of condemnation, it confirms their condemnation."[64] So, Ra's seems to fit the profile of the power of the law, specifically as it

---

[60] Matt. 3:17 (NRSV).

[61] Rom. 2:12 (NRSV).

[62] Rom. 4:15 (NRSV).

[63] Gal. 3:10 (NRSV).

[64] Douglas Moo, *The Epistle to the Romans* (Grand Rapids: Wm. B. Eerdmans Publishing Company, 1996), 277.

condemns humanity.

Additionally, Ra's is like Satan because not only is Satan at war with Christ, but he also comes to accuse and destroy human beings. Satan is not interested in forgiveness or redemption; his only intent is to bring condemnation and death. In the Old Testament, for example, Satan approaches God to tear down Job, as well as to condemn Joshua, the high priest.[65] In fact, in Greek, the word Σατανας *(Satanas)* means adversary or enemy, and the Greek word διαβολος *(diabolos)*, from where we get the word "devil," literally means accuser. This profile accurately fits Ra's—an adversary and accuser of the people of Gotham. William Mounce writes, "The works of the devil are always painful and many times subtle. He longs to bring suffering . . . even to the point of death."[66] Satan accuses the people of God, and he frequently uses the power of the law to bring guilt, shame, and indictment. Indeed, the law is how he has a stronghold over humanity because people fail to keep the law. It is worth pointing out that in this way penal substitution is compatible with Christus victor. As Tom Schreiner writes, "Penal substitution reminds us that sinners are enslaved to demonic powers because of our own moral failure and guilt."[67] In other words, human corruption

---

[65] Job 1-2; Zechariah 3 (NRSV).

[66] William Mounce, *Complete Expository Dictionary of Old and New Testament Words* (Grand Rapids: Zondervan, 2006), 179.

[67] Thomas Schreiner, "Penal Substitution View" in *The Nature of the Atonement: Four Views*, ed. James Beilby and Paul Eddy (Downers Grove, IL:

serves as the means for the devil to oppress humanity. Likewise, Ra's Al Ghul is deceptive and treacherous, and he holds the law over the people of Gotham oppressively due to their moral failures. Indeed, the reason that he comes to Gotham is to bring down the smite of destruction in the name of justice.

Ra's Al Ghul tells Bruce, "It should be you standing by my side saving the world."[68] Interestingly, Ra's thinks that Bruce is properly justified in bringing down the sword of condemnation on the people of Gotham. Ra's Al Ghul recognizes Bruce Wayne's moral righteousness, and hence his set-apartness from the people of Gotham. He does not toss Bruce in with the rest of Gotham city because he understands that he is not like its corrupt citizens; he is different to them. However, Bruce Wayne tells Ra's Al Ghul, "I will be standing where I belong: between you and the people of Gotham."[69] Bruce acts as a mediator; he is the Christ-figure, the one who stands in the gap.[70] Jesus' role as mediator is essential to the doctrine of atonement. As Paul writes in 1 Timothy 2:5, "There is one mediator . . . Christ Jesus, himself human . . . who gave himself a ransom for all." Like Christ, Batman takes the

---

IVP Academic, 2006), 68.

[68] *Batman Begins*, directed by Christopher Nolan (2005; Burbank, CA: Warner Home Video, 2005), DVD.

[69] Ibid.

[70] Interestingly, when Bruce Wayne says this, a giant wooden beam falls horizontally onto Bruce and pins him down, an image that corresponds to Jesus nailed to the wooden cross as he atones for the sins of humanity and battles the powers of evil.

oncoming blow of judgment onto himself, rather than allowing it to fall on the men and women of his city. Although Bruce is one of the people of Gotham, in a way greater he is greater than them. Therefore, he is properly suited to be a mediator on their behalf because he can serve as their representative while standing on a higher plane to offer the people salvation. Apart from Christ's role as mediator, the power of the law and Satan would bring down the smite of condemnation on humanity. However, Jesus Christ is humanity's mediator. William Mounce writes "Since there is only one mediator . . . all people are united under that oneness and all people should be offered the benefit of Christ's ransom."[71] Likewise, through Batman's victory, the people of Gotham receive the benefits of Batman's triumph because he acts as a mediating representative. They are liberated from the judgment of Ra's Al Ghul. In the same way that Batman delivers Gotham from the power of Ra's Al Ghul, Christ also liberates humanity from the oppressive power of the law. Paul affirms this in Romans 8:2, "Christ Jesus sets you free from the law of sin and death," and again in Galatians 3:13, "Christ redeemed us from the curse of the law." The power of the law no longer effectively condemns the people of God because of what Christ did on the cross. Just as Christ is victorious as humanity's mediator over the powers and principalities, so too Batman advocates on behalf of the people of

---

[71] William Mounce, *Pastoral Epistles* (Nashville: Thomas Nelson, 1999), 87.

Gotham, and renders those who might oppress them powerless.

In summary, *Batman Begins* illustrates both the Christus Victor and substitutionary models of the atonement. The city is in bondage, and under the oppression of various powers like Falcone and Ra's Al Ghul. However, Batman disempowers these villainous forces. He takes on the cause of Gotham city, and he becomes a representative who receives the judgment for the people of Gotham. Batman triumphs over the powers, and ultimately saves the people of Gotham.

## The Dark Knight: Taking Our Place

*"For our sake he made him to be sin who knew no sin, so that in him we might become the righteousness of God."*
*2 Corinthians 5:21*

In *The Dark Knight*, the story picks up a few months after *Batman Begins* leaves off. The film introduces the Joker, a sociopath who is intent on disrupting harmony and justice and bringing disorder and chaos. The Joker makes a deal with the crime bosses to kill Batman if they pay him an enormous amount of money. Meanwhile, Batman and Jim Gordon work together to get rid of organized crime in Gotham, and they include District Attorney Harvey Dent, an honest and noble person, in their plans. The Joker continues to terrorize Gotham, and publicly demands that Batman reveal his identity, threatening to otherwise murder more people. The Joker targets Harvey Dent, and ultimately captures him, and ties him and his partner Rachel to oil drums and explosives. Batman is able to save Dent, but Rachel dies. Harvey goes mad after the loss of Rachel, and he begins to question his efforts to restore Gotham. The Joker approaches Dent and tells him to abandon his law abiding ways, and to "introduce a little anarchy." Dent accepts the Joker's advice, and he proceeds to go on a vendetta against the people who have wronged him. Batman confronts the Joker, and the Joker explains to Batman how Dent's corruption will devastate the people of Gotham. The Joker predicts that Dent's fall will ruin any hopes of cleaning up the city. Batman ultimately captures the Joker, and hands him over to the police, only to discover that the former district attorney has indeed lost his moral uprightness, and is responsible for the murder of five people. Dent kidnaps Jim Gordon and his family, but Batman arrives to protect everyone, and Dent plummets to his own death. In the final scene, Batman decides that he himself will take the responsibility for Dent's crimes, so that Dent's righteous standing is not ruined, and in order to restore peace to Gotham. Gordon reluctantly agrees to Batman's plan, and signals to hunt down Batman, who flees into the night.[72]

## Atonement in *The Dark Knight*

As with *Batman Begins*, the underlining thread that runs through *The Dark Knight* is the restoration of Gotham city. Again, the city of Gotham serves as a picture of the entire world. It is fallen, corrupt, and in desperate need of saving. In *The Dark Knight*, the audience is introduced to district attorney Harvey Dent, a

---

[72] *The Dark Knight*, directed by Christopher Nolan (2008; Burbank, CA: Warner Home Video, 2008), DVD.

representative of the people of Gotham. He possesses moral integrity, uprightness, and he is an outstanding citizen, if not the prime Gothamite. As Jim Gordon tells Dent, "We all know you're Gotham's white knight."[73] Harvey Dent stands for everything good and noble, and Batman desires for Dent to lead Gotham into a state of flourishing. Bruce Wayne is impressed and pleased by Harvey's uprightness, and sees him as the type of person who could properly lead and steward the city. Bruce publicly declares, "I believe in Harvey Dent. I believe on his watch, Gotham can feel a little more safe, and a little more optimistic."[74] Ultimately, Bruce hopes to entrust the care of Gotham into Dent's hands. Not only does Batman recognize Dent's moral authority but the people of Gotham do as well. The mayor tells Dent, "The public likes you. But that means it's on you. Are you up to it? You better be. They get anything back on you, those criminals will be back on the streets."[75] Naturally, as a moral exemplar and leader of the city, Dent is targeted as one of the Joker's primary victims to destroy, either by killing him, or by tarnishing his character. Ultimately, the Joker succeeds in the latter, thereby thwarting Batman's initial hopes for Dent.

There are distinct parallels between Harvey Dent and Adam, (and consequently every human who is represented in

---

[73] *The Dark Knight*, directed by Christopher Nolan (2008; Burbank, CA: Warner Home Video, 2008), DVD.
[74] Ibid.
[75] Ibid.

Adam—created for righteousness and leadership—but falls). First, both Adam and Harvey Dent begin in a state of moral righteousness. Second, both Adam and Harvey Dent serve as representatives for a larger people. Finally, both Adam and Dent fall from their original state, which negatively effects the people they represent. Adam is the ultimate human being, created to steward the earth, and lead humanity. As Genesis 1:27-28 says, "So God created humankind . . . and God said to them, 'fill the earth and subdue it; and have dominion.'" Adam begins his existence in a state of complete innocence, and God has certain hopes and desires for Adam, the prime human. However, Adam is tempted by Satan, and chooses to act in evil and self-serving ways. Adam disregards God and the law of God, and he recreates right and wrong for himself. As Karl Barth notes, "From the time of Adam it had been man's sin to want to become and be his own judge."[76] Similarly, Wayne Grudem says, "Their sin struck at the basis for moral standards, for it gave a different answer to the question, 'What is right?'"[77] As a result of Adam's fall, all of humanity is broken. Paul writes, "Sin came into the world through one man, and death came through sin, and so death spread to all because all have sinned."[78] Adam's corruption results in consequences for all of humanity. Like Adam, Harvey Dent starts

---

[76] Karl Barth, *CD* IV.1 (Peabody, MA: Hendrickson Publishers, 1956), 258.
[77] Wayne Gruden, *Systematic Theology* (Grand Rapids: Zondervan, 1994), 493.
[78] Rom. 5:12 (NRSV).

off as a virtuous and upright character. Indeed, Dent is the prime Gothamite, and an ideal citizen; he is noble and ready to lead Gotham into a bright future.  Nevertheless, he gives in to the Joker's temptation, and experiences a fall (Dent literally falls and dies, just as Adam's fall leads to his death). With the fall of Harvey, the entire city of Gotham is ruined because Harvey, an elected official, represents the people of Gotham. Harvey's fall nullifies not only his moral deeds, but also his efforts to lead Gotham, and to put away criminals and mobsters. As Jim Gordon says, "All of Harvey's prosecutions, everything he fought for: undone. We bet it all on him. The Joker took the best of us and tore him down. People will lose hope."[79]  Therefore, both Adam and Dent share in the problem of human transgression and guilt. Although they both begin in a state of righteousness, they deviate from the role originally intended and hoped for them.[80]

If Harvey Dent is Adam, then the Joker is undoubtedly Satan. The Joker's likeness to Satan can be demonstrated in three ways. First, the Joker intends to destroy human beings, and to cause trouble for Batman in every way possible, especially if it

---

[79] *The Dark Knight*, directed by Christopher Nolan (2008; Burbank, CA: Warner Home Video, 2008), DVD.

[80] Another interesting similarity worth considering is that Harvey Dent is a man of the law; he is the district attorney of Gotham. Nevertheless, in spite of all of his efforts to keep and uphold the law, he fails, paralleling the NT teaching that legal righteousness or works through the law can never lead to salvation. Hence, the need for Christ, who fulfills the law perfectly, and saves the world.

means terrorizing the people whom Batman cares about. As John 10:10 says, "The thief comes only to steal and kill and destroy." The Joker pursues this same destructive mission. Second, the Joker has no moral compass. Jesus describes the devil in John 8:44: "He was a murderer from the beginning and does not stand in the truth, because there is no truth in him." In the same manner, the Joker is purely evil, and possesses no amount of good or redeemable qualities. His primary desire is to excavate the worst in people, and to lead them to kill and destroy each other. The Joker tells Batman, "When the chips are down, these civilized people will eat each other."[81] Indeed, the Joker continually tempts Batman throughout the film. This is the third way the Joker is like Satan: the Joker tempts both Batman and Harvey Dent to act contrary to their morally upright nature. Batman tells the Joker, "I have one rule," and the Joker responds, "Well, then, that's the rule you'll have to break. The only sensible way to live in this world is without rules, and tonight you're going to break your one rule." Batman says, "I'm considering it."[82] This statement demonstrates that Batman experiences true temptation, but does not succumb to it. In the final exchange between Batman and the Joker, Batman throws the Joker off a high building. The Joker laughs triumphantly while he plummets to the ground because he thinks

---

[81] *The Dark Knight*, directed by Christopher Nolan (2008; Burbank, CA: Warner Home Video, 2008), DVD.
[82] Ibid.

he has successfully corrupted Batman; however, Batman catches the Joker with his grappling gun before he hits the ground, and pulls him back up. The frustrated Joker says, "You just couldn't let me go, could you? You truly are incorruptible."[83] While Dent gives in to the lures of the Joker, Batman overcomes the Joker's temptation. This parallels the temptations of Adam in the Garden, and Christ in the desert; Satan approaches them both, but Jesus is the second and greater Adam. Christ is the new and worthy representative to lead humanity into righteousness. As Norval Geldenhuys writes,

> To Adam also, the first man, the opportunity was given to choose between good and evil while his inward nature was still intact. In his case also, the temptation came from without. And yet he fell, with all the fatal results of that Fall. Christ, however, who had come as Head of the new humanity, was victorious over all the attacks of the powers of darkness.[84]

Adam and Harvey Dent act contrary to the good, and instead, act in a self-serving manner in the hopes that they will empower themselves. In contrast, Batman, like Jesus, is on a mission to carry out truth and justice, and he does not seek to glorify himself, nor to satisfy his own indulgences.

Given Batman's likeness to Christ, how does Batman atone

---

[83] *The Dark Knight*, directed by Christopher Nolan (2008; Burbank, CA: Warner Home Video, 2008), DVD.

[84] Norval Geldenhuys, *Commentary on The Gospel of Luke* (Grand Rapids: Wm. B. Eerdmans, 1960), 157.

for Gotham in *The Dark Knight?* First, he offers himself as an example of moral goodness and love. Batman's desire from the beginning of his mission is to follow in the footsteps of his father and restore the city. Alfred tells Bruce, "Your father…believed that his example could inspire the wealthy of Gotham to save their city." Bruce asks, "Did it?" Alfred replies, "In a way. Their murder shocked the wealthy and the powerful into action." Bruce concludes, "People need dramatic experiences to shake them out of apathy."[85] Hence, Bruce assumes the persona of Batman as a way to inspire people toward justice and kindness. At the beginning of the *The Dark Knight*, Batman encounters "copy-cats" who dress up like Batman and try to fight criminals. However, they end up doing more harm than good. There is only one true Batman, and he is the only one person who can assume the role to save the city. Although the copycats' intentions to imitate Batman may be good, their execution is not right. When Alfred sarcastically suggests that Bruce hire the copy-cats, Bruce responds, "That isn't what I had in mind when I said that I wanted to inspire people." Evidently, Bruce hopes to bring about change in the city through his own example. Initially, the people of Gotham do not comprehend the spirit behind Batman's acts; however, the citizens of Gotham gradually understand what it means to imitate Batman's example. This is evident when the

---

85 *Batman Begins*, directed by Christopher Nolan (2005; Burbank, CA: Warner Home Video, 2005), DVD.

Joker captures one of the copycats and taunts him, asking, "Why do you dress up like Batman?" and the man responds, "He's a symbol that we don't have to be afraid of scum like you."[86] The man begins to understand that imitating Batman is more to do with being transformed internally, than changing his external appearance; moreover, it means living free from the oppression of fear. Later in the story, the Joker installs bombs on two ferries full of people, one carrying civilians, and the other transporting prisoners. He gives a detonator to the passengers on each boat, provoking them to destroy the other boat, threatening to otherwise explode both ferries. The passengers on the ferries are faced with a heavy dilemma: to act in self-preservation and yield to the demands of the Joker, or to make the morally good choice of love and sacrifice, and hope that evil will not succeed. Although tempted, the passengers do not choose to blow each other up, but anxiously wait to see what will happen. They are now transformed by the spirit of the sacrificial and good Batman hero; through Batman's example, they are saved. The Joker watches, expectant that the people will kill each other, but they do not, and he becomes visibly upset. As the Joker prepares to take matters into his own hands and blow up the boats, Batman intervenes and prevents him. The scene demonstrates that the distorted and selfish desires of Gotham's citizens do not dominate them as they

---

86 *The Dark Knight*, directed by Christopher Nolan (2008; Burbank, CA: Warner Home Video, 2008), DVD.

previously did. The great, moral model of Batman transforms people into better human beings. As the Joker hangs upside down from Batman's rope, confident that the people will yield to lawlessness, Batman retorts, "This city just showed you that it is full of people ready to believe in good!"[87] Evidently, Batman's example inspires the people of Gotham to act morally and in love, rather than in fear and selfishness.

Batman's impact on the people of Gotham highlights the moral exemplar motif of the atonement found in Scripture. Batman's example is so powerful that it drives fear out of people, and fills their hearts with sacrificial love. As 2 Timothy 1:7 says, "For God has not given us a spirit of fear . . . but of love." Similarly, 1 John 4:18 says, "Perfect love casts out fear." Batman inspires people to be transformed from within, and this is how the copycat and passengers on the ferry withstand the terror of the Joker. Likewise, Christ lives a perfect life, full of love and goodness. He exhorts people not to live in fear, and he gives humanity the power to walk in love. Jesus teaches to forgive, sacrifice, and to love each another. In fact, Jesus even teaches people to love their enemies. Interestingly, the people on the ferries are literally enemies; one ferry carries civilians, and the other carries criminals. Both parties are at enmity with each other. Nevertheless, both groups of people miraculously choose to act

---

[87] *The Dark Knight*, directed by Christopher Nolan (2008; Burbank, CA: Warner Home Video, 2008), DVD.

in love toward their enemies. They model the extreme love Christ teaches. Ultimately, Jesus demonstrates the highest expression of love by laying down his life on the cross. Due to his great love, Jesus undergoes immense pain and suffering for humanity. Likewise, Batman manifests his love for the people of Gotham by undergoing grueling pain night after night as he fights against injustice. Instead of abandoning people to destroy themselves, both Batman and God provide a perfect example of how human beings ought to live redemptively, and not destructively. In this way, both Batman and Jesus bring salvation to the world; they get humanity back on the right track by exemplary lives of love and sacrifice.

Second, Batman atones for Gotham in that he serves as Dent's substitute; Batman bears the weight of Dent's punishment despite his own innocence. By the end of the story, Batman faces the problem of Harvey's fall from right moral standing. Gotham's white knight, the city's shining example of righteousness, the ideal citizen who was supposedly ready to lead the city, experiences a horrible moral failure, and as a consequence, the entire city is heading for ruin. The criminals whom Harvey put away will be released, and the people will fall into despair. The people of Gotham put their faith in the one who was supposed to represent them, but Dent was not the man of integrity everyone thought he was. Corruption and chaos will be rampant throughout. If the city falls due to Dent's failure, then the Joker's plan succeeds, resulting also in Batman's failure. However, Batman hates evil too much to allow the Joker to succeed in his plan. He longs to restore justice to the city due to his great love for the people of Gotham. In fact, it is nearly impossible for Batman not to do something to ensure that harmony returns to Gotham, because simply walking away "would be unfitting and unworthy of Himself."[88] So, Batman provides a plan: he himself will assume the responsibility for Harvey's murders, thereby safe-guarding Harvey's righteousness, and keeping Gotham safe. Batman says, "The Joker cannot win. . . . I'm not a hero unlike Dent, I killed those people. That's what I can be." James Gordon retorts, "No. You can't! You're not!" Batman responds, "I'm whatever Gotham needs me to be . . . You'll hunt me. You'll condemn me."[89]  The innocent Batman takes the blame for Dent's transgressions, and the caped crusader rides away.

Perhaps nowhere else in the Batman films is the Christian doctrine of atonement most clearly illustrated than in the final moments of *The Dark Knight*. Batman models Christ's atoning work in that he substitutes himself in the place of the guilty, and bears the penalty on behalf of sinners. Hence, theologians call this model of atonement "penal substitution." There are a number of different observations worth noting in this scene as it relates to

---

[88] St. Athanasius, *On the Incarnation*, (Crestwood, NY: St. Vladmir's Seminary Press, 1946), 32.

[89] *The Dark Knight*, directed by Christopher Nolan (2008; Burbank, CA: Warner Home Video, 2008), DVD.

penal substitution.

First, like Christ, Batman is innocent, not guilty. Neither Batman nor Christ have done anything to indict themselves; they are truly good. Although Batman and Jesus are legitimately tempted, they do not yield to temptation, and they commit no wrong. The writer of Hebrews says that Christ is, "one who in every respect has been tempted as we are, yet without sin."[90] As Batman runs away in the final moments of the film, Jim Gordon's son asks, "Why is he running, dad?" Gordon responds, "Because we have to chase him." The boy rightly observes, "He didn't do anything wrong."[91] This statement parallels what others affirmed when they witnessed Jesus' death. The criminal besides Jesus says, "He received the same sentence we did, but he has done no wrong,"[92] and, intriguingly, a Roman centurion at the crucifixion states, "Glory be to God. Certainly, this was a righteous man."[93] As Paul explains what happened on the cross, he describes Jesus as "him who knew no sin."[94] Like Christ, Batman commits no transgression; he is innocent.

Second, both Batman and Christ choose to become substitutes in the place of sinners. While at times Batman works to save the city by solving the problem of systemic evil, in *The*

---

[90] Heb. 4:15 (NRSV).
[91] *The Dark Knight*, directed by Christopher Nolan (2008; Burbank, CA: Warner Home Video, 2008), DVD.
[92] Luke 23:41 (GNT).
[93] Luke 23:47 (NIV).
[94] 2 Cor. 5:21 (NRSV).

*Dark Knight*, Batman also concerns himself with the sins of an individual man, as he takes them upon himself. And since both Batman and Christ are innocent, and morally righteous, they are properly suited to stand in the place of those who are unrighteous, because as Philip Hughes notes, "only He who was entirely without sin of His own was free to bear the sin of others."[95] When Batman says, "I killed those people," the crimes of Dent are transferred on to Batman in a similar fashion that the sin and guilt of Adam (and therefore all of humanity), is transferred onto Christ.[96] As 1 Peter 2:24 says, "He himself bore our sins in His body on the cross," and in 1 Peter 3:18 it says, "For Christ also suffered for sins once for all, the righteous for the unrighteous, in order to bring you to God." The New Testament writers recognized that when Christ died on the cross, he actually took the place of sinful people, in order to rescue humanity from their former sentence. In the New Testament, Paul writes, "God made him who knew no sin to be sin."[97] In some way, on the cross, the sins of the world were attached to Christ. Wayne Grudem explains, "This does not mean that God thought that Christ had himself committed the sins, or that Christ himself actually had a

---

[95] Philip Hughes, *The Second Epistle to the Corinthians* (Grand Rapids: Wm. B. Eerdmans,1962), 213.

[96] The Old Testament establishes and explains the importance of the sacrificial system and one of the primary motifs in Old Testament sacrifices was substitution. For more on this see, Thomas Schreiner's essay "Penal Substitution View" in *The Nature of the Atonement: Four Views.*

[97] 2 Cor.5:21(NRSV).

sinful nature, but rather that the guilt for our sins (that is, the liability to punishment) was thought of by God as belonging to Christ rather than to us."[98] Philip Hughes beautifully explains Christ's substitution: "As all mankind are . . . lost sinners, we hold that Christ is their only righteousness, since, by His obedience, He has wiped off our transgressions . . . by His blood washed away our stains, by His cross borne our curse, and by His death made satisfaction for us."[99]

Third, both Batman and Christ experience condemnation as a result of their substitutionary act.[100] On the cross, Jesus experienced the condemnation and wrath that was due for sinners. The book of Isaiah foretells Christ's suffering, "But he was wounded for our transgressions, crushed for our iniquities, upon him was the punishment that made us whole."[101] Through his act of substitution, Jesus bears the judgment of sinners, just as Batman bears Harvey's judgment when he tells the police commissioner, "You'll condemn me . . . because that's what needs to happen." This is the penal aspect of penal substitution. Batman

---

[98] Wayne Gruden, *Systematic Theology* (Grand Rapids: Zondervan, 1994), 574.

[99] Philip Hughes, *The Second Epistle to the Corinthians* (Grand Rapids: Wm. B. Eerdmans,1962), 212.

[100] In traditional accounts of penal substitution, God the Father plays the role as the one who pours out his wrath. On the one hand, Batman assumes the role of God the Father because the condemnation is a self-imposed condemnation, on the other hand Commissioner Gordon acts as God the Father because he is in partnership or union with Batman to achieve the same goal—the restoration of justice and harmony—but his role is to condemn Batman.

[101] Is. 53 (NRSV).

pays the price for Harvey's transgressions. The police hunt down Batman, and deem him a criminal. Similarly, when the sins of the world are laid on Jesus Christ, he is condemned as an outcast. As Karl Barth says, Jesus is the "rejected one" and "the judge judged in our place."[102] Barth writes,

> What took place is that the Son of God fulfilled the righteous judgment on us men by Himself taking our place as man and in our place undergoing the judgment under which we had passed. . . . Everything happened to us exactly as it had to happen, but because God willed to execute His judgment on us in His Son it all happened in His person, as His accusation and condemnation and destruction. He judged, and it was the Judge who was judged, who let Himself be judged.[103]

Although condemnation could justifiably be poured out on humanity, God chooses a different way. Both Batman and Christ possess such great love for human beings that they are personally willing to undergo judgement, in order to save people.

Fourth, both Batman and Christ serve as new and greater representatives than the ones who come before. Harvey Dent and Adam fail in their designated roles as representatives of the people, hence, a new representative is necessary who can fulfill the role properly. The New Testament describes Christ as the new representative for humanity. Paul writes,

> For if the many died through the one man's trespass, much more surely have the grace of God and the free gift in the

---

[102] Karl Barth, *CD* II.2 (Peabody, MA: Hendrickson Publishers, 1956), 346.
[103] Karl Barth, *CD* IV. 1 (Peabody, MA: Hendrickson Publishers, 1956), 222.

grace of the one man, Jesus Christ, abounded for the many. . . . Therefore just as one man's trespass led to condemnation for all, so one man's act of righteousness leads to justification and life for all. For just as by the one man's disobedience the many were made sinners, so by the one man's obedience the many will be made righteous.[104]

Batman looks upon the problem of sin in Gotham, and the fallen state of its representative, Harvey Dent, and he becomes sin in order to empower Harvey and restore Gotham to what it should be.[105] However, the key point here is that the salvation of Gotham objectively rests on Batman himself. He, and he alone accomplishes the work. He is the greater representative to Harvey, the one who achieves what Harvey cannot; Batman restores harmony to Gotham.

Fifth, both Batman and Christ achieve victory through substitutionary atonement. Jeremy Treat writes, "How is Satan defeated? Christ defeats (Christus Victor) by removing the ground of Satan's accusation, which Jesus does by paying the penalty for sin (penal substitution)."[106] The Joker stands to accuse Harvey and Gotham of their failures. If he succeeds in tearing down Gotham, then he wins the battle for Gotham's soul. However, Batman solves the problem of Harvey's failure by offering himself as

---

[104] Rom. 5:15, 18-19 (NRSV).

[105] This has an Eastern Orthodox flavor to in that God sees the plight of humanity, and so He sinks down to become human in order to raise humanity back up to its proper state.

[106] Jeremy Treat, *The Crucified King* (Grand Rapids: Zondervan, 2014), 204.

substitute, thereby defeating the Joker's plan, and claiming the status of victory and hero. This is precisely what Christ does on the cross. Paul writes, "And when you were dead in trespasses . . . God made you alive . . . erasing the record that stood against us with its legal demands. He set this aside, nailing it to the cross. He disarmed the rulers and authorities and made a public example of them, triumphing over them in it."[107] Jesus triumphs over the rulers and authorities by nullifying the sins of humanity; likewise, Batman triumphs over the evil Joker by taking away the transgressions of Harvey. At the end of the movie, Batman is victorious.

In summary, the final moments of *The Dark Knight* are rich in theological imagery that should not be ignored. The story vividly illustrates Christ's atoning work; it highlights the moral exemplar, penal substitution, and Christus Victor motifs of the Christian doctrine of atonement. Batman inspires the citizens of Gotham through his example, and through it they are saved. Additionally, Batman bears the penalty of Harvey's transgression—illustrating penal substitution—by which Batman is victorious over the powers of evil.

---

[107] Col. 2:13-15 (NRSV).

# The Dark Knight Rises: Defeating the Strong Man

*"When I am lifted up from the earth, I will draw all people to myself."*
*John 12:32*

*The Dark Knight Rises* takes places eight years after the events of *The Dark Knight.* The people of Gotham experience relatively safe living conditions. Trouble begins when a mercenary named Bane, who has taken over The League of Shadows, arrives in Gotham to fulfill the will of Ra's Al Ghul. Bruce, who has not ventured out as Batman for the past eight years, discovers Bane's arrival and decides to return to Gotham as its protector. Batman learns of Bane's intricate plan to take over Wayne Enterprises, and to steal his technological resources, one of which includes a nuclear fusion reactor that can be turned into a time bomb. Batman enlists the help of Selina Kyle, an acrobatic jewel thief, to help him stop Bane, but she betrays him. Batman engages in an intense hand-to-hand fight with Bane, but Bane is too strong and breaks Batman's back. Bane puts Bruce in an underground prison cell, and tells him that once he destroys Gotham, he will kill Bruce. Bane returns to Gotham, and takes over the city completely. He destroys the bridges, blocks anyone from leaving or entering the city, buries the police department in the sewers, and releases criminals from a high security prison. Moreover, Bane threatens the city with a bomb that he stole from Wayne Enterprises. Via television in the bottom of the cell, Bruce painfully watches Bane terrorize Gotham. Meanwhile, Bruce regains his strength, and successfully climbs out of the prison pit. Bruce returns to Gotham, and pursues Bane once more. Batman defeats Bane with the help of Selina Kyle. He discovers that the only way to stop the bomb from destroying the city is to fly it out over the bay. So Batman carries the bomb away from the city, and it explodes over the ocean. Everyone believes that both Bruce Wayne and Batman are dead, but the film ends with the revelation that Bruce is still alive.[108]

## Atonement in *The Dark Knight Rises*

As with the previous films, Gotham city is a microcosm for humankind. The city's initial prosperity and serenity resembles the state of humanity in Eden. All is well in Gotham until, like in Eden, something evil creeps in that seeks to destroy the people.

Bane, like the previous villains in the Batman films, depicts the powers of evil, specifically the devil and the power of death. If Batman is like Christ, then Bane, the adversary, properly fits the

---

[108] *The Dark Knight Rises*, directed by Christopher Nolan (2012; Burbank, CA: Warner Home Video, 2012), DVD.

role of the devil. Bane is known for his terrifying physical strength. He overcomes many of his opponents who are like small animals before him. His overwhelming strength makes him a unique villain. Interestingly, the gospels describe Satan as the "strong man," who needs to be immobilized; Jesus is the one who immobilizes the strong man.[109] Bane does not blatantly reveal himself to people, but instead sneaks into Gotham through the sewers. The caution of 1 Peter 5:8 is appropriate here: "Discipline yourselves, keep alert. Like a roaring lion your adversary the devil prowls around, looking for someone to devour." Peter's illustration of the devil as a lion is also fitting for Bane who covers his mouth with a mask that looks like the iron teeth of a beast. Moreover, Bane and his henchmen dwell underground. Their domain parallels the tradition of Satan's dwelling in the sphere of hell below, and both villains seek to conquer the people who dwell on earth. The citizens of Gotham have clearly grown too comfortable, unsuspecting, and unvigilant, and are therefore easily overtaken by Bane when he captures the city.[110] When Bane seizes the city, he acts as the lord or ruler of Gotham. The New Testament writers describe Satan as "the god of this age" and the "ruler of the world,"[111] and Bane dictates the entire city in a similar fashion to Satan's rule over the world.

---

[109] Matt. 12:29 (NRSV).

[110] At first, many doubt that Bane is real, which is similar to the problem of the modern person who does not believe that the devil exists.

[111] 2 Cor. 4:4, John 12:31 (NRSV).

Closely related to Bane's likeness to Satan is his similarity to the power of death. According to Hebrews 2:14, the devil has the power of death.  This is relevant in the case of Bane, who possesses a device that can bring death to the people of Gotham—through a neutron bomb, he can blow up the entire city at any moment. Bane also represents the power of death because he is a menacing and destructive force, who crushes people mercilessly, and kills without hesitation. His fighting style is intended to inflict the most amount of pain in the most efficient way possible.

How is Batman like Christ, and how does he demonstrate the work of atonement? First, Batman combats and exhausts the powers of evil, and triumphs over them. That is to say, the forces of evil spend their energy trying to defeat Batman, but fail. Batman first encounters Bane in the sewers, and the two immediately engage in a physical combat.[112] However, Bane, the stronger fighter, tells Batman that he plans to invade, and take over Gotham and Wayne Enterprises, which Bane calls his "home."[113] Similarly, Satan hopes to rule the nations of the world, thereby making the world his home.[114] However, God will not permit

---

[112] As Batman is about to engage with Bane, Selina Kyle distances herself from Batman out of concern for her own life. She denies knowing him—similar to when Peter denies knowing Christ for fear of losing his own life out of association with Jesus.
[113] *The Dark Knight Rises*, directed by Christopher Nolan (2012; Burbank, CA: Warner Home Video, 2012), DVD.
[114] Rev. 20:8 (NRSV).

Satan to lord over the world, so he intervenes through Christ to ensure that the evil one does not step his territory. This is precisely what Batman does; he does not want to see Bane and his henchmen take over the city, so he engages him in battle to stop him. But the menacing Bane grabs Batman, and breaks his back. This moment in the story might seem like a defeat for Batman, but in fact puts Bane on the path to defeat; by tearing down Batman, Bane actually strengthens him, hence ensuring Bane's future demise. This very battle is the means for Batman's ultimate victory. Likewise, Jesus understood that he was going to battle with Satan on the cross, and that he would be killed on the cross. Nevertheless, in John he says, "The hour has come for the son of man to be glorified. . . . Now the ruler of this world will be driven out."[115] Jesus perceived his death on the cross to be the act that conquers the rulers of the world.

Interestingly, Jesus also says, "Now is the time for the son of man to be lifted up."[116] Here, Jesus refers to being literally lifted up on the cross—the very thing that destroys him. But he also refers to his ultimate glorified state which he achieves by dying on the cross. This is significant because it parallels the scene in which Bane physically lifts up Batman to break his back, and in the end, brings Batman more glory. As Gustaf Aulen points out, evil "loses

---

[115] John 12:23, 31 (NRSV).
[116] Ibid.

the battle at the moment when it seems to be victorious."[117]

After Bane breaks Bruce's back, he is lowered into the pit. This scene corresponds to Christ's burial in a grave after his death. However, neither men remain below the earth.  As it is written in Psalm 16: 10, "For you will not abandon my soul to Sheol, or let your holy one see corruption." Jesus emerges victorious out of the grave, more powerful than ever. Similarly, during Bruce's time in the underground pit, he builds himself up so that he is even stronger than before. Bruce grows so strong that he accomplishes the nearly impossible climb out of the pit. As he ascends from the pit, the other captives shout and cheer, "Rise! Rise!"[118] The risen Bruce then lowers a rope into the pit to free the other captives. Bruce's rise out of the pit ensures the liberation of Bane's other victims. Christ's resurrection has similar effects; having risen and conquered death, so too can others be raised and be given freedom. Isaiah 42:7 foretells Christ's activity: "You will free the captives from prison, releasing those who sit in dark dungeons."

The strengthened Batman returns to Gotham, and battles Bane once more, but this time, Batman overcomes Bane. He breaks open the mask that administers Bane painkillers, thereby depleting his strength, leaving him powerless to fight. Likewise, Jesus strips the power from the forces of evil. N.T. Wright

---

[117] Gustaf Aulen, *Christus Victor* (London: SPCK, 1931), 55.
[118] *The Dark Knight Rises*, directed by Christopher Nolan (2012; Burbank, CA: Warner Home Video, 2012), DVD.

explains, "All the powers of the world including sin and death and violence themselves did their worst to Jesus, and that force was exhausted."[119] Through the resurrection, Jesus makes a laughing stock out of the powers evil. He disempowers them through his victory over the cross. Not even death and the grave can hold him down. As Gustaf Aulen says, "The resurrection is . . . first of all the manifestation of the decisive victory over the powers of evil which was won on the cross."[120] Jesus takes the evil powers by surprise. Like the forces of evil, Bane does not expect Batman to return. When Bane sees the bat symbol light up again with fire, he is visibly shocked, and says, "Impossible!" Baffled, he later asks, "I broke you. How have you escaped?"[121] By defeating Bane, Batman frees Gotham; he removes Bane from his position as lord over Gotham, thereby liberating the people from his reign of terror, just as Jesus Christ defeats the strong man who held humanity in bondage. St. Iranaeus writes, "But through the second man he bound the strong one and spoiled his goods and annihilated death bringing life to man who had become subject to death."[122]

As Batman defeats Bane, he declares, "You have my

---

119 N.T. Wright, *Atonement: The Contemporary Debate* (Interviewed by St. Johns) Accessed April 22, 2015, http://www.youtube.com/watch?v=gi_ixf7YxCo
120 Gustaf Aulen, *Christus Victor* (London: SPCK, 1931), 32.
121 *The Dark Knight Rises*, directed by Christopher Nolan (2012; Burbank, CA: Warner Home Video, 2012), DVD.
122 St. Iranaeus, *Against Heresies III.23* Accessed April 22, 2015, http://www.ccel.org/ccel/schaff/anf01.ix.iv.xxiv.html

permission to die."[123] This is what God will tell the devil and the powers of evil on the last day. God has allowed evil to go about for God's purposes, but there will come a time when God completely vanquishes the powers that oppress humankind. As Paul writes in Romans 16:20, "God will soon crush Satan," and Revelation 20:10 says, "The devil who had deceived them was thrown into the lake of fire and . . . will be tormented day and night forever and ever." God's people can rest in the hope that God will soon eradicated all evil.

Second, Batman atones for Gotham in that he acts as a substitute; he swallows up the judgment of death and evil, and carries it up on himself. The atomic bomb is a symbol of death over the people of Gotham; it is Bane's tool of judgment for their transgressions. However, like Christ, Batman's mission is to stop the works of evil. As 1 John 3:8 says, "The Son of God appeared for this purpose, to destroy the works of the devil." Batman is the only one who can properly deal with the bomb. He attaches it to his plane and flies it away from the city, so that only he is affected by it. Batman becomes Gotham's representative, and stands for the people, mediating on their behalf. Batman takes upon himself the judgment that was intended for Gotham. He willingly offers up his life so that the city is saved; apart from Batman's actions, millions of lives would have been destroyed. Similarly, God

---

[123] *The Dark Knight Rises*, directed by Christopher Nolan (2012; Burbank, CA: Warner Home Video, 2012), DVD.

intervenes in Christ to save his people from the judgment of death. As St. Athanasius says, "For the human race would have perished utterly had not the Lord and Savior of all the Son of God come up among us to put an end to death."[124] Moreover, like Christ, Batman takes upon himself the weight of judgment and saves the city. When Catwoman pleads with Batman saying, "Save yourself, you don't owe these people any more. You've given them everything." Batman responds, "Not everything. Not yet," implying that he is yet to lay down his very life for the people of Gotham.[125] Like Batman, God owes humanity nothing. He is self-sufficient, and does not need to bestow anything on the world. Nevertheless, Jesus says he has come, "not to be served but to serve, and to give his life a ransom for many."[126] The judgment of death rests upon humankind, but Christ carries it upon himself. Through God's work on the cross and resurrection, death itself is ultimately vanquished. As Paul writes, "'Death has been swallowed up in victory. Where, O death, is your victory? Where, O death, is your sting?' thanks be to God! He gives us the victory through our Lord Jesus Christ."[127]

In summary, *The Dark Knight Rises* possesses many significant parallels to the Christ event. The film also illustrates the

---

[124] St. Athanasius, *On the Incarnation*, (Crestwood, NY: St. Vladmir's Seminary Press, 1946), 35.
[125] *The Dark Knight Rises*, directed by Christopher Nolan (2012; Burbank, CA: Warner Home Video, 2012), DVD.
[126] Mark 10:45 (NRSV).
[127] 1 Cor. 15 (NRSV).

Christus Victor model of atonement. The powers of evil hold humanity in bondage, but like Christ, Batman exhausts these powers, and liberates human beings. Ultimately, Batman offers his own life to save Gotham from death.

## Sharing the Good News

*"I am not ashamed of the gospel, because it is the power
of God that brings salvation to everyone who believes."*

Romans 1:16


*The Dark Knight Trilogy* has grossed over two billion dollars worldwide.[128] *The Dark Knight* is in the top five voted best films of all time, and its companion films are in the top one hundred.[129] People everywhere are captivated by the Batman story. It is not only at the cinema that people demonstrate their enthusiasm for Batman; over 130,000 people regularly attend Comic-Con (an annual gathering to celebrate comic book culture in San Diego). At this event, hundreds of people wait in line for several hours to take photos of their favorite hero's costume, or to catch a preview of the latest comic book film, set to release in theaters. Those in attendance even dress up like Batman, or other superheroes from comic book stories. Lest one thinks that superheroes are just for children, it should be noted that primarily adult men and women

---

[128] "Box Office History for Batman Movies," *The Numbers,* Accessed April 22, 2015 http://www.the-numbers.com/movies/franchise/Batman.
[129] "IMDB Charts Top 250," *IMDB,* Accessed April 22, 2015, http://www.imdb.com/chart/top.

attend these comic conventions around the nation. Christians have something to say to those who are taken with the Batman mythology, but are not yet followers of Jesus: "One who is greater than Batman is here."

The message of Batman is a message for Christians as well. The thought of Jesus dying for my sins, or the atonement as penal substitution, frequently feels like a far removed reality; Christians often have difficulty understanding what happened other than simply recognizing that it was a significant event. Jesus dying on the cross might be a nice item to check off on the list to check of important things to believe, yet sadly, it possesses very little existential significance for many believers today. There is a way to remedy this problem. Christians who go to the movies to watch the Batman films, and leave feeling exhilarated and emotionally impacted, can know that the stories illustrate what Christ has done for humanity; they can thereby redirect their affections to Christ, who is the proper object of those emotions.

The good stories of a culture should not be forgotten, and Batman is a good story because it points to The Great Story. What Batman does imperfectly, Christ does perfectly. What Batman does in part, Christ does in full. Christians should be glad for the success and cultural impact of Nolan's *Dark Knight Trilogy* because the films powerfully illustrate what Christ accomplished on the cross. Indeed, this is what the message of Christianity is about: Jesus Christ came into the world to save sinners.

# *Appendix:*

# *Christ's Two Natures*

Batman is a type of Jesus. That is the thesis of this book, and I primarily focused on the doctrine of atonement to support this claim by contending that Batman and Christ both provide atonement for people, and both characters restore justice, peace, and harmony. I want to briefly consider one more way in which Batman and Jesus are similar, and this entails looking at the two natures of Christ.

One of the common puzzles people wrestle with in regards to the Christian faith is the doctrine of the incarnation. This is the Christian teaching that God, specifically the second person of the Trinity, became a man. However, if one pauses to think about the incarnation for a moment, it seems immediately nonsensical. How can God turn into a mere man? How can a divine being become a human being? How can God, who is inherently other, set apart, and unique, change into something that is opposite to himself?

Isn't this this blatantly self-contradictory?

In order to better address these issues, we need to turn to the early church fathers, specifically Cyril of Alexandria, and the council at Chalcedon. Cyril of Alexandria, a pastor from the fifth century, understood the puzzle that the doctrine of the incarnation presents. He rightly contended that the proper way to think about the incarnation is that Jesus Christ possesses two natures: divine and human. Cyril writes,

> It is incumbent on us to be true to these statements and teachings and to comprehend what is meant by saying that the Logos from God took flesh and became human. We do not say that Logos became flesh by having his nature changed, nor for that matter that he was transformed into a complete human being composed out of soul and body. On the contrary, we say that in an unspeakable and incomprehensible way, the Logos united to himself in his hypostasis, flesh enlivened by a rational soul, and in this way became a human being.[130]

So it is not so much that God the Son turns himself into something opposite to himself, or something that he is not. To borrow Cyril's word, God does not "transform" into man. Rather, the second person of the Trinity takes on an additional nature to the one he already possesses, so that he now possesses two natures: divine and human. In other words, although each of us has a human nature, there is a perfect union of divine nature and

---

[130] Cyril of Alexandria, "Cyril of Alexandria's Second Letter to Nestorius" in *Christological Controversies* edited by Richard Norris (Philadelphia: Fortress, 1980), 132.

human nature in the person of Jesus Christ. In AD 451, the council of Chalcedon built upon Cyril's understanding of the two natures of Christ and provided for us the following helpful definition. They wrote,

> Following, then, the holy Fathers, we all unanimously teach that our Lord Jesus Christ is to us One and the same Son, the Self-same Perfect in Godhead, the Self-same Perfect in Manhood; truly God and truly Man; the Self-same of a rational soul and body; co-essential with the Father according to the Godhead, the Self-same co-essential with us according to the Manhood; like us in all things, sin apart; before the ages begotten of the Father as to the Godhead, but in the last days, the Self-same, for us and for our salvation . . . acknowledged in Two Natures unconfusedly, unchangeably, indivisibly, inseparably; the difference of the Natures being in no way removed because of the Union, but rather the properties of each Nature being preserved, and (both) concurring into One Person and One Hypostasis; not as though He were parted or divided into Two Persons, but One and the Self-same Son and Only-begotten God, Word, Lord, Jesus Christ.

Hence, in the one person of Christ, the two natures, divine and human, remain distinct, yet somehow perfectly united. This is what is called the hypostatic union.

So what does all of this have to do with Batman? Batman is a man just like Jesus Christ. Bruce is one of us, but he is also greater than us. Batman is like Jesus, in that he also possesses two natures: a supernatural/transcendent nature, and a human/mortal nature. When Bruce Wayne becomes Batman, he does not transform himself into something that he is not; he does not become that which is opposite to himself. Rather, he takes to himself an additional nature, a transcendent, "bat-hero" nature in order to accomplish the task at hand while retaining his identity as the ordinary man, Bruce Wayne. The human nature is evident in the man who appears at Wayne Manor, attends social events, confides in his butler, and so forth. The superhero nature is evident in the one who wears the cape and cowl, protects vulnerable citizens, fights criminals, etc.[131] The two natures come together paradoxically in one person. As Bruce says, "As a man, I'm flesh and blood, I can be ignored, I can be destroyed; but as a symbol... as a symbol I can be incorruptible, I can be everlasting."[132] So too, the second person of the Trinity takes on an additional nature to accomplish the task of reconciliation. God the Son uses the human nature as a tool; he becomes a human being in order to exemplify righteousness, to die for the world, and hence, to save it. As Athanasius writes, "He, the Mighty One, the Artificer of all, Himself prepared this body . . . and took it for His very own, as the instrument through which He was known and in which He dwelt."[133] Bruce acts similarly in that he knows that in order to truly help the people of Gotham, he needs to assume a second nature. As Paul Levitz says, "Batman is a tool he

---

[131] To be clear, any action of Bruce Wayne's is an action of Batman's (and vice versa) because they are one and the same person.

[132] *Batman Begins*, directed by Christopher Nolan (2005; Burbank, CA: Warner Home Video, 2005), DVD.

[133] St. Athanasius, *On the Incarnation*, (Crestwood, NY: St. Vladmir's Seminary Press, 1946), 34.

puts on to accomplish what he needs to do."[134]

Christ, in his very essence, being God, takes on the identity of a servant. Bruce Wayne, a billionaire of high esteem, takes on the anonymous identity of a crime fighter. God the Son becomes a man, and Bruce Wayne becomes Batman. The heroes humble themselves, and assume another nature in order to accomplish their mission, and they ultimately sacrifice their lives to ensure humanity's salvation.

---

[134] *Batman Unmasked*, written by Steven Smith (2008; Burbank, CA: Warner Home Video, 2008), TV Movie.

# *Bibliography*


Anselm. "Why God Became Man." In *The Major Work* edited
by Brian Davis and G.R. Evans, 25-356. Oxford:
Oxford University Press, 2008.

Athanasius. *On the Incarnation.* Crestwood, NY: St. Vladmir's
Seminary Press, 1946.

Aulen, Gustaf. *Christus Victor: An Historical Study of the Three Main
Types of the Idea of Atonement.* Translated by A.G. Herbert.
New York: Macmillan, 1951.

Baker, Mark and Joel Green. *Recovering the Scandal of the Cross:
Atonement in New Testament        and Contemporary Contexts.*
Downers Grove, IL: InterVarsity Press, 2003.

Barth, Karl. *Church Dogmatics.* 4 vols. in 13 parts. Edited by
Geoffery Bromiley & Thomas F. Torrance. Peabody, MA:
Hendrickson Publishers, 1956.

*Batman Begins.* Directed by Christopher Nolan. 2005. Burbank,
CA: Warner Home Video, 2005. DVD.

*Batman Unmasked.* Written by Steven Smith. 2008. Burbank, CA:
Warner Home Video, 2008. TV Movie.

Beilby, James and Paul Eddy (eds). *The Nature of the Atonement:
Four Views.* Downers Grove, IL: IVP Academic, 2006.

Beilby, James and Paul Eddy. "The Atonement: An
        Introduction." In *The Nature of the Atonement: Four Views*,
        edited by James Beilby and Paul Eddy, 9-22. Downers
        Grove, IL: IVP Academic, 2006.

"*Box Office History* for Batman Movies," *The Numbers*, Accessed
        April 22, 2015,
        http://www.thenumbers.com/movies/franchise/Batman.
Calvin, John. *Institutes of the Christian Religion*. Peabody:
        Hendrickson, 2007.

Craig, William. "Can We Be Good Without God," *Reasonable
        Faith*. Accessed March 17, 2015.
        http://www.reasonablefaith.org/can-we-be-good-
        without-god.

Crisp, Oliver. *Roundtable Discussion on Analytic Theology*.
        Interviewed by Center for Philosophy of Religion.
        Accessed March 19, 2015.
        http://philreligion.nd.edu/videos/round-table-
        discussions.

Cyril of Alexandria. "Cyril of Alexandria's Second Letter to
        Nestorius." In *The Christological Controversy*, edited by    Richard
Norris Jr., 131-135. Philadelphia: Fortress Press,        1980.

Davis, Stephen. *Christian Philosophical Theology*. New York:
        Oxford University Press, 2006.

Detweiler, Craig, and Barry Taylor. *A Matrix of Meaning: Finding
        God in Pop Culture*. Grand Rapids: Baker Academic, 2003.

Dodd, C.H. *The Parables of the Kingdom*. London: Nisbet, 1936.

Erickson, Millard. *Christian Theology*. Grand Rapids: Baker Books,
        1998.

Garrett, James. *Systematic Theology: Volume 2*. Grand Rapids: Wm
        B. Eerdmans Publishing Co., 1995.

Geldenhuys, Norval. *Commentary on The Gospel of Luke.* Grand Rapids: Wm. B. Eerdmans, 1960.

*Good News Bible.* New York: American Bible Society, 1976.

Grudem, Wayne. *Systematic Theology.* Grand Rapids: Zondervan, 1994.

Hart, Trevor. "Redemption and Fall." In *The Cambridge Companion to Christian Doctrine.* Edited by Colin Gunton, 158-188. Cambridge: Cambridge University Press, 1997.

Hauerwas, Stanley and L. Gregory Jones. "Introduction: Why Narrative?" In *Why Narrative,* edited by Stanley Hauerwas and L. Gregory Jones, 1-18. Eugene, OR: Wipf and Stock, 1997.

*Holy Bible: New International Version.* Grand Rapids: Zondervan, 2011.

*Holy Bible: New Revised Standard Version.* San Francisco: Harper Collins Publishers, 1989.

Hughes, Philip. *The Second Epistle to the Corinthians.* Grand Rapids: Wm. B. Eerdmans,1962.

"IMDB Charts Top 250," *IMDB,* Accessed April 22, 2015, http://www.imdb.com/chart/top.

Iranaeus. *Against Heresies III.23.* Accessed April 22, 2015. http://www.ccel.org/ccel/schaff/anf01.ix.iv.xxiv.html.

Lewis, C.S. "On Stories." In *Essays Presented to Charles Williams,* edited by. C.S. Lewis, Grand Rapids: Eerdmans, 1966.

Marsh, Clive, and Gaye Ortiz (eds). *Explorations in Theology and Film.* Hoboken, NJ: Wiley-Blackwell, 1997.

McKnight, Scot. *A Community Called Atonement.* Nashville, TN: Abingdon Press, 2007.

Moo, Douglas. *The Epistle to the Romans*. Grand Rapids: Wm. B.
     Eerdmans Publishing Company, 1996.

Morris, Leon. *The Atonement*. Downers Grove, IL: InterVarsity
     Press, 1984.

Mounce, William *Complete Expository Dictionary of Old and New
     Testament Words*. Grand Rapids: Zondervan, 2006.

Mounce, William. *Pastoral Epistles*. Nashville: Thomas Nelson,
     1999.

Oropeza, John (ed.) *The Gospel According to Superheroes*. New
     York: Peter Lang International Academic Publishers,
     2006.

Porter, Stephen. "Rethinking the Logic of Penal Substitution."
     In *Philosophy of Religion: A Reader and Guide* edited by
     William Lane Craig, 596-608. New Brunswick: Rutgers
     University Press, 2002.

Quinn, Philip. "Abelard on Atonement: 'Nothing Unintelligible,
     Arbitrary, Illogical, or Immoral about It'." In *Reasoned
     Faith: Essays in Philosophical Theology in Honor of Norman
     Kretzmann*, edited by Eleonore Stump, 153-177. Ithaca,
     NY: Cornell University Press, 1993.

Rea, Michael. "Philosophy and Christian Theology." *Stanford
     Encyclopedia of Philosophy*. Accessed March 17, 2015.
     http://plato.stanford.edu/entries/christiantheology-
     philosophy.

Russell, Bertrand. "A Free Man's Worship." In *Why I Am Not a
     Christian*, edited by Bertrand Russell, 104-116. London:
     Allen and Unwin, 1957.

"Safe," in *Beware the Batman*. Directed by Sam Liu. Burbank,
     CA: Warner Bros Animation, 2013.

Schreiner, Thomas. "Penal Substitution View." In *The Nature of the Atonement: Four Views,* edited by James Beilby and Paul Eddy, 67-98. Downers Grove, IL: IVP Academic, 2006.

Skelton, Stephen. *The Gospel According to the World's Greatest Superhero.* Eugene, OR: Harvest House Publishers, 2006.

Stott, John. *The Cross of Christ.* Leicester: InterVarsity Press, 1986.

Tallon, Felix and Jerry Walls. "Superman and Kingdom Come: The Surprise of Philosophical Theology." In *Philosophy for Superheroes,* edited by Tom Morris and Matt Morris, 207-220. Chicago: Open Court, 2005.

*The Dark Knight Rises.* Directed by Christopher Nolan. 2012. Burbank, CA: Warner Home Video, 2012. DVD.

*The Dark Knight.* Directed by Christopher Nolan. 2008. Burbank, CA: Warner Home Video, 2008. DVD.

Treat, Jeremy. *The Crucified King: Atonement and Kingdom in Biblical and Systematic Theology.* Grand Rapids: Zondervan, 2014.

Vidu, Adonis. *Atonement, Law, and Justice.* Grand Rapids: Baker Academic, 2014.

Vos, Geerhardus. *Redemptive History and Biblical Interpretation.* Phillipsburg, NJ: Presbyterian and Reformed Publishing Co., 1980.

White, Mark (ed). *Batman and Philosophy.* Hoboken, NJ: John Wiley and Sons, 2008.

Wright, N.T. *Atonement: The Contemporary Debate.* By St. John's Nottingham. Accessed April. 22, 2015. http://www.youtube.com/watch?v=gi_ixf7YxCo.

Wright, N.T. *The New Testament and the People of God.* Minneapolis: Fortress Press, 1992.

## *About the Author*

Shebuel Varghese is a graduate of Gordon Conwell Theological Seminary. He is a visiting professor of theology at Peniel Bible Seminary in India, and he blogs at faithcolloquium.com.

Made in the USA
Lexington, KY
01 July 2017